RANDOM FANTASIES AND NIGHTMARES

Random Fantasies and Nightmares

C. GAFF

 Printed in the United States of America. First Printing, 2022. Ebook ISBN: 978-1-7364789-4-3; Paperback ISBN: 978-1-7364789-5-0, 7:13 Publishing.

I dedicate this book to my parents and the family, teachers, and childhood friends that helped me to realize my potential over the years, whether directly or indirectly.

You were the reasons why I had enough to fill a whole book. Whether a person had a positive or negative part in my life, it did give me the drive and emotion to write.

Thank you.

Side Notes:

1. A lot of these pieces were written when I was very young, I did not change them, I printed them the way I found them. I wanted to show where I began and the development of my craft over the years.

2. Some of the more current short stories in this book are unfinished, because they were the beginnings of full novels. I may eventually go back and finish them; however I make no guarantees.

Enjoy!

CONTENTS

THE WAY, WAY BACK

(Works Pre-2002)

The Ghost of the Blood Signed Letter

(SHORT STORY - WRITTEN IN 1997, FOR AN 8TH GRADE ENGLISH ASSIGNMENT. THE ONLY EDITS MADE WERE THOSE THAT THE TEACHER MADE...THOUGH SHE DID MISS A FEW, THAT I NOTICED.)

June 12, 1874

"James get in here, she's going again!" Mrs. Larson carefully held her sixteen-year-old daughter while she painfully convulsed. Rebecca had been sick for months now, Dr. Dennom had diagnosed her with an unknown illness and told the Larsons she hadn't long to live. Just months ago she was an average sixteen-year-old girl, she was extremely beautiful, yet now only a mirror image of her former self. Her long blond hair was now so ratted that nearly a year would go by before they could ever get it out. Her brown suntanned skin was now a pale white, except for the red around her eyes and in her cheeks. Her room that used to smell of soft perfumes, roses, and wild flowers, now smelled of sickness, camphor oil and body odor. No one was allowed to see her, her own parents scarcely went into her room, for fear of catching this mysterious disease. Then one day Rebecca asked for something to write with. Her mother quickly got it and left the room, as instructed by Rebecca. She wrote, using great strength just to hold the pen. Then upon finishing she folded it in letter form, she took her candle and lt the wax drip onto the paper nicely sealing it. Then taking the quill of the pen and slit her index finger, writing her name in blood on the front. Finishing her letter she ripped a piece of cloth off of her bed sheet, wrapping it around her finger to stop the blood. With great pain and struggle she lifted herself from the bed. She walked unsteadily and as if fainting fell to the floor in the corner of the room. She pulled a nail in the floor board to reveal a compartment holding a small brass key. She then pulled herself to the other side of the room. A small hole in the wall proved to be the lock in which the key belonged. She slipped the key in, turned it to the right, and the door cracked open. She pulled it open to reveal a room with beautifully carved furniture, a stained glass lamp hanging over a carved marble fireplace, gorgeous hand woven rugs, and beautiful tapestries had been placed carefully about the room. She set the letter facing up on the solid oak carved table. She put the door and the key pack in their place, hidden from the world, her only secret. Later that day, she died, not telling a soul.

123 Years Later

July 5, 1997

Ben set the box down on the floor of the kitchen. The house smelled of old newspapers, strong perfumes, and misty furniture. He walked into the living room, nothing but a fireplace stood in the room. It was a plain brick fireplace, nothing fancy really. The floor was covered with a green carpet, which smelled as if a dog had lain there and rotted. At the side of the room, the carpet had unraveled a little revealing a beautiful hard wood floor. Ben, curious to see why it had been cover, pulled the carpet up more, sure that his mom

would replace it anyway. He pulled until half of the floor was revealed. The planks so carefully placed, were all in perfect shape. Not even one squeak! Excited to find such an awesome historical treasure, he ripped up the rest of the carpet. He rolled it up, almost choking on its putrid smell. He carried it outside to the rented trash bin. When putting the carpet into the rubbish, Ben heard his mother running toward him.
"Ben what are you doing?" She asked heatedly. "I thought this should have a proper resting place, it's been rotting in that house for years!"
"Why? That was good carpet!"
"You're kidding me, aren't you?"
No, really it was."
"Yeah, sure, if you like the smell of rotten dog!"
She pulled up the lid, , it didn't take her long to say "Oh my...where was it?"
"In the living room, wait till you see what was underneath!"
Ben's mom walked into the house, she gasped as she walked into the living room, "It's so beautiful!" She dropped to the floor and caressed the grain of the wood. "Why would someone want to cover this?"
"I don't know, but it had to be for some reason, I guess."
He walked toward the stairs.
"Did anyone ever come up here, all the doors are boarded up and there's cobwebs everywhere?!"
"I don't know, it was an older couple, maybe they couldn't get up the steps very well!" She shouted up the stairs while directing the movers. He went up to one of the doors and said "Hey mom, is it okay if I tear some of these boards off?"
"Sure honey, but try not to hurt the walls or anything!"

"Yeah, I'll try not to!" he shouted down the stairs.

The first room, the door was hard to open, there was an old broken chair at the corner of the room with dust and webs all over it. The smell of dust in his nostrils made him sneeze. He shut the door and went to the next room, the next room smelled of rotting flesh and in the middle of it was a dead raccoon. He could tell it was, because of the black, brown, and gray fur still rotting off the stale carcass. Ben shut the door as fast as he could. Then moved on to the next room, there were extra boards on the door, it took all of his strength to pull them off. As he pushed open the door the pungent aroma of flowers and perfume filled the air. There was a beautiful canopy bed in one side of the room, next to it was a simple dresser with a mirror built on top. On the dresser was a flask of purple colored perfume, a vase of wildflowers, and an antique looking hairbrush. The room had a faint pink glow, as if it were a vison of his imagination. Yet everything was so real that not a doubt in his mind could convince him otherwise. Suddenly, something brushed his shoulder. He turned. He saw the most beautiful girl he had ever seen before. She smiled at him as she reached out for him, he took her hand.

Then all at once a feeling of warmth and comfort seized him. She had told him everything about herself, yet not said a word. He, being a sixteen year old guy, was very attracted to her from the moment he saw her. She took him into her room. Somehow the room which had been so beautiful before, was now lost within her radiance. She took him to her dresser. She pulled a single rose from the vase and gave it to him. He took it from her. His hand left hers and everything went dark. As his eyes got adjusted he saw he was in the hallway, the door to his back, in his hand he was clutching a rose. He knew he hadn't imagined the room, the girl, or the rose. He opened the door again and saw an astonishing sight, the room was empty space. With a sigh of loneliness he shut the door. He leaned back with his head against the door, wondering if he would ever see the mysterious girl again.

All through the night he couldn't stop thinking about her. Her touch, her long blond hair, her dark perfect skin, and the rose she had given him. Was he in love with her? Was she a ghost? Was she trying to tell him something? His mind pulsed with thoughts about her.

"Hey Ben, snap out of it!" his mother said as she snapped, her fingers in front of his face, "You're going to be late for the first day at your new school!" Ben holding a spoonful of cereal jumped as he heard his mom's voice. "Ben, are you okay, you've been acting kinda weird!?"

"Yeah, sure mom, I'm fine, see ya," he said walking quickly out the door to his car. He started the car and switched on the radio to Y101. Not aware of where he was going he drove to the Crystal Cemetery. He walked through the gate, as if knowing where to go he trodded toward the grave of :

Rebecca Larson
Feb. 14th, 1858 – June 12, 1874
Age 16, In loving memory of her
father, mother, and 3 siblings,
killed of scarlet fever, may her
soul rest peacefully for eternity.

He could barely read it, yet knew exactly what it said. As if waking from a trance, all at once he realized where he was and where he should have been.

He ran back to his car knowing how late he was going to be. He played the words of the stone over and over in his mind. Knowing that she was the girl he had seen yesterday, but his heart was not wanting to believe the truth.

At school the classes flew by, barely hearing a word the teachers said. Days went by, Ben was still enchanted by the ghostly image of Rebecca Larson who died over 100 years ago. Every night he would go to her room finding nothing but dust and cobwebs.

Then one night, in a dream, he found a key under a floorboard and slipped it into a hold in the wall to reveal…he woke up. It was very early in the morning, the sun was creeping over the treetops. He went to the window, and looked at all the dark houses. He knew everyone was still asleep.

Then the aroma of roses again filled the air, and he knew he wasn't alone. He turned, there she was dressed in white. In her hair were the reddish roses he had ever seen. Her deep blue eyes pierced his heart as a sad expression appeared on her face. "Rebecca, I…" he started, as soon as he started speaking she put her finger to his lips, signaling him to quiet. She stared deep into his eyes, and by some unethical force, they were pulled together, in a kiss that would melt even the coldest of hearts. She pulled away hesitantly not wanting to ever end the magical moment. She took his hand, and let him to her room. Ben still dazed by the kiss, would never forget how sweet her lips had tasted, wanting to take her back into his arms and never let go. Yet, he couldn't, he knew she could never really be part of his life, although she was his life and everything in it. Ben not realizing where they were going was led to the wall and she opened it up. Ben now noticing where he was, looked the secret room over. He walked over to the table and picked up the letter. Suddenly , he realized she was gone the only trace of her was the letter he held in his hand.

He clutched it as if, when he let go his life would crumble into little pieces of forgotten memories and dreams. He knew with more than anything he'd ever known before that he would never see her again. He could barely read the letter for the tears welling up in his eyes. It said:

Dearest Benjamin,

I love you! I will never forget you. You must not give in to your pain, we will soon be together, but not now. I shall haunt this house no more. Good-bye.

Love always, Rebecca

Ben, leaning against the wall he had recently put back, slid to the floor holding the letter tightly in his hand as tears poured down his face. He felt he would never survive without her, yet knew some how he had to.

The ghost of Rebecca Larson was never seen again. To this day only Ben and Rebecca share the secret beauty of her empty room holds. The letter he put back on the table along with his own. No one will ever know what it said, but will always be remembered from generation to generation. A story of how true love can not be separated by time, by death, not by any other earthly force, yet can only be united by two.

The Power Within

(SCREENPLAY - STILL UNFINISHED. WRITTEN A FEW YEARS AFTER THE GHOST OF THE BLOOD SIGNED LETTER, APPROXIMATELY 1998.)

[Camera begins on a wasteland, completely barren]

[As the speaker talks, the camera slowly scans the area, revealing crashed planes, abandoned guns, skeletons in U.S. Army attire, and the remains of a few crumbling structures.]

Speaker: This, the reconstruction of Earth, is 2090. The past had brought the 3rd World War and so plummeted the planet into extreme poverty and despair. Never more can there be mass destruction at the push of a button…for those buttons have all been pushed and these the days after, and in these days after, not only the thoughts of human kind have been changed, but their genetic makeup. The radiation of these great nuclear bombs has taken its toll on the people, thus producing things that were, until now, unimaginable…

[Loud boom, black screen.]

[Fading into picture, woman screaming in labor.]

[Nuclear plant, everyone is wearing protective clothing, except for the woman that has thrown hers to the side to have her baby.]

Speaker: On this day a baby was born…

[Watch as baby is born.]

Speaker:…and this child would someday change the world.

[Man in protective clothing pulls the baby out as the

room starts to glow, stops glowing when the baby is in the man's arms.]

[Camera falls on mother who is not moving, eyes closed.]

[Music, credits, title. Black screen, white words.]

[Loud noise as camera focuses on a large, white building. This is the lab where Alexander is behind held, white letters at the bottom of the screen flash: February 5, 2112.]

[Camera on Alexander enclosed in a glass room, people in white lab jackets watch him, he is pacing the room.]

[He looks at the people, then back at the floor.]

[Suddenly he falls to the floor, people in the white jackets race around on the outside. One person comes into the room with protective gear on, checks Alexander's pulse. Alexander grabs his hand, gets him by the neck, and pulls his protective head gear off. Now you can see the man's face, he is scared. Alexander still has him by the neck, his arm wrapped around the man's neck. Alexander looks through the glass his white hair tossed and his white eyes raging, tiny lightning bolts flicker through them. He puts his other hand lose to the man's exposed head. He stares straight at another man on the outside, who seems to be in charge. He is wearing a suit.]

Alexander: It is time, Dr. Cross...you know what I can do...you've seen it...when I was born...all your stupid tests...I'm through with your games...I'm not an animal...

[Seems to be getting out of breath.]

Dr. Cross: What are you going to do out there, how are you going to get the energy to survive? We take care of you here, you're safe here...

[Alexander gets angry.]

Alexander: I'm a lab rat here! I've never seen the sun or the grass…

[Pushes the scared man up against the glass.]

Alexander: And if you would like to see this man go home to his family…I would…suggest…that you let me out…of here!

[Alexander badly out of breath.]

[Dr. Cross slowly goes to the door and opens it.]

[Alexander walks through it, the scared man still in his arms, the whole while staring at Dr. Cross.]

Alexander: Now get in there…all of you!

[They do as he says, so that he doesn't kill the scared man. Alexander closes the door and locks it behind them. Alexander puts his hand on the scared man's head, closes his eyes. The scared man starts to shake and Alexander starts to glow. The scared man falls to the floor, Alexander looks at Dr. Cross. Camera on Cross, then back at Alexander. Alexander looks down at the man on the floor, then to the door of the lab. Something jingles. Alexander looks back at Dr. Cross. Camera on Cross. Cross is jingling some keys. Alexander gets a scared look and bolts directly toward the door. Cross fumbles with the keys and the door. Finally gets it open. Looks at the exit door. Camera on the door, it is swinging, and Alexander is gone. Cross feels for the scared man's pulse. Looks back up at the door. Camera on door. Close up of Cross.]

Cross: He's alive…barely…

[Part 2]

[Loud rock music, small apartment, cluttered. Clothes on the floor, take out boxes, man in bed. No blankets, they've been thrown on the floor. He stirs. Rolls over to face the camera. Sits up on the edge of the bed, scratches his head, and gets up. Walks into the kitchen, picks up a box of Chinese takeout, smells it, frowns, puts it back on the table. Looks into the fridge. The phone rings. Walks up to the phone and picks it up.]

Anderson: Anderson

[Listens into the phone for a minute.]

Anderson: I'm on vacation...I don't care if it is...it can wait...what do you mean now? Yeah, fine. [Angry.] Yeah, I'll be there.

[Clicks the phone off, then throws it across the room, very angry.]

(Unfinished. Minimal changes for spelling and grammar. Written in 1997, when I was fourteen years old.)

August 13, 2090

Angelina Romaine, single mother of three and one to come, clocked into her shift. She walked down the long shafter to the end where she found her protective clothing. She put it on being careful to seal every crack. The suit was big on her, whoever had made them hadn't taken pregnancy into account. It was a good job though, she knew the work, and unlike most jobs out there today, she could afford to keep her children. She loved them all. There wasn't anything she wouldn't do for them: Adrianna; Marcella; Terresa; and soon Alexander. He was to be her only son. Oh how happy her husband would have been to see her bear a son. He had been gone for almost eight months now, she had accepted the fact that he had probably been killed like thousands of other husbands, fathers, brothers. But her son would grow, and he would be something great.

She had felt strange that morning; however, Alexander wasn't due for another ten days. All her other children had been right on time, so she did not see the need to take off work.

*(**Character development notes, unknown date.)*

Name: Alexander Romain

Birth Date: Friday, August 13, 2090 (Due actually August 23, 2090)

Birth Place: Salem, OR (Nuclear Reactor Plant)

Mother: Angeline Romaine

Other: Being born, he was exposed to pure nuclear energy, which changed his chromosomal makeup, making his body so that it could not make its own energy. Therefore he would have to get his energy from others to stay alive, being born took too much of his energy and he inadvertently killed his mother by taking her own energy. After birth, he was taken to a lab where he was kept for all of his young life, studying him. Until one day in 2112, when he was tired of living his life in a "cage". He broke out of the lab and into the real world. Living in the lab had meant no emotional stimuli which resulted in little to no emotion. On the street, Alexander killed to survive. He had to take the energy of others to sustain his own energy. He soon learned from a nosy reporter (Shannon), that there could be a cure for his disease. The only cure was in a nuclear wasteland, that none had entered after the war. There, as rumor has it, is the only everlasting power. A small orb, made from technology that had never been charted contained the strength and charge of an everlasting lightning bolt. The wasteland is located on the late city of New Orleans. During the war, this orb was to explode, creating a mass tremor through the earth that would tear it apart. To Alexander, this energy would be enough to last his body through eternity. However, because this energy had not been studied and no one knows its real power, instead of giving him the energy he so desperately needs it could serve its original purpose and the earth would be no more.

Name: Shannon DeSoto
Birth Date: June 30, 2091
Birth Place: Sacramento, CA (Mercy Hospital)
Other: She is a very nosy reporter who always wants to get the first "story". After hearing that Alexander had escaped, she tracked him down and almost got herself killed by him. She tells him about the possible cure, so he spares her. She has come with him on his journey, leading him to the reactor site. As time passes, she shows him what life is about and how wonderful the world can be. In the end, they feel something for each other that Alexander never thought he could feel, love.

Chris & Michelle

(POETRY 1998)

Michelle and Chris, after school, a small town,
It's Friday night and their listenin' for the sound
Of people talking 'bout the party tonight,
And it's like a carnival with neon lights,
They overhear, eight is when the party starts,
They'll be there, pick up some drinks from Wal-Mart,
'Cause Chris has been to the parties before,
He's drank a lot, till he's been on the floor,
Michelle doesn't drink, but she's along for the ride,
She's Chris's girl, so she'll stay by his side,
They get there, Chris says things'll be alright.
Michelle's not sure, but she don't want to fight,
So inside they go, every is sayin', "Hi"
There's a band, and a keg to their right,
There's nothing wrong here, it seems to Michelle,
Her inhibitions fall, and her morals fail,
She picks up a cup and drinks it all down and
She feels so high, she doesn't want to land,
It comes so soon that the party is over,
Chris is wasted so he gives the keys to her,
Michelle grabs up the keys, and stumbles to the car,
She shouldn't be driving, but they're not going far,
She starts up the care and they pull away,
It's all okay, till they get to the highway,
She barely sees the headlights coming near,

And as they hit, silence is all she hears,
They're in the ditch, Chris's eyes are closed,
There's blood on his face and all over his clothes,
She takes his hand, but it hurts to move her head,
His hand's getting cold and she knows he's dead.
She's getting tired, wants to close her eyes,
Then comes the sirens and the red and blue lights.

Tears of Fire

(POETRY – WRITTEN IN 1999, PUBLISHED UNDER THE PEN NAME F0XF1R3_V1X0N IN 2007)

Your words stay in my mind
They tear at me like knives
I'm hysterically crying
It's ripping me up inside

I remember your soft kisses
And the way you touched my hair
The way we went everywhere
And all they could do was stare

We were the perfect couple
Everyone said it to be so
I thought you would always be there
I never thought you'd go

You took my heart with you
When you went away
You said you'd come back
You said it would be soon someday

Now I've gotten your letter
You told me that you loved me
You said that you were coming home
You'd be here in time for tea

But next to it the truth
So sad, but oh so true
The Army they regret to inform
that I won't be seeing you

They told me why you're gone
and that you served your country
They said I should be proud
You died protecting me
I understood their words
but I really did not care
I wanted you back again
My life with you to share

Speaking of the Truth

(POETRY - WRITTEN IN 1999 AFTER A BAD BREAKUP, PUBLISHED IN 2007 UNDER THE PEN NAME F0XF1R3_V1X0N)

Tell me of your truths
Tell me of your lies
Look at me with your cold
and blood shot eyes

I see your actions before me
I listen to what you say
Little by little you deceive me
Little by little I pay

I held you in my heart
You held me in your arms
I fell in love with you
And all of your sweet charms

I knew it wouldn't last
I really should have known
That it would be to hard for you
To find and use the phone

I sat here in my room
Waiting for your call
I waited for two weeks
And then finally I saw

I went right there to see you
I knew it should be soon
I really had to do it
I had to get over you

You blamed it all on me
If I cared I would have phoned
You were to busy to pick it up
As you spent your day at home
But now you are out of my life
Again I'll never see you
But I still care about you so
I wish you luck in all you do.

Crimson Waves

(POETRY - WRITTEN AFTER A BAD BREAKUP IN 1999, PUBLISHED IN 2006 UNDER THE PEN NAME F0XF1R3_V1X0N.)

Shiny blade of steel
In my tiny hand
Crimson puddles spread
Over cold and whitened sand
The love of ages fades
As I watch the bloody waves
Carry you to sea
To your cold and watery grave
I saw you with another
You held her and kissed her cheek
I was just so upset
To you I couldn't speak
I lured you to the beach
To where the sea and moon they tie
I waited until you got there
To ask you about your lies
You explained them all to me
In your words...on confusion
I listened to you
But know it was only an illusion
I came to you, one hand within my pocket
You didn't see me as I took this tiny sword
and slashed your spine
One gesture, without a word

You looked at me in disbelief
As you staggered to your knees
You wiped your hand behind your neck
Observing death's crimson fees
And now I stand here watching you
Your last breaths of life I see
For now it will all be true
That in the end you loved only me.

THE LITTLE WAY BACK

(Works 2003-2017)

Admon Yue Malik

(CHARACTER PROFILE – CREATION DATE: 2007 - FEATURED IN THE ARCHIVES OF METAPHYSICAL WARFARE: VOLUME 1: THE END IS THE BEGINNING IS THE END)

Full Name: Admon Yue Malik
Age: Unknown, looks late teens/early 20's
Gender: Male
Race: Nepa'Daem
Marital Status: Uninterested
Spawn: Navar Yue Malik
Height: 5'7" [Human Form] 7' [True Form]
Weight: 347lbs. (Body Mass Compacted)
Hair Color: Bright Red
Eye Color: Crimson
Scars/Tattoos: No Scars/A Few Red Tribal Tattoos
Alignment: True Evil
Companions: None
Allies: Few
Enemies: Many
Description: Admon Yue Malik in human form shows little of his evil nature. His bright red hair, deep red eyes surrounded by dark circles, and sharp shark-like teeth are the only features that show any traces of his true nature. In true form, Admon is a towering seven foot tall, with the lower body of a scorpion. Admon is much heavier than he appears, because of the endoskeleton beneath his human-like skin.
Armor/Weapons: The armor of the scorpion encases his

tender internal organs, protecting them. [In a fight, it is much harder to pierce through the endoskeleton. Admon's skin can be cut and he will bleed with a successful hit, but his internal organs cannot be reached easily.] Admon's weapon of choice tends to be his staff. This staff, it's name Anima'Bacculum, is no ordinary staff. Burned into this staff are magical insignias of his people, long gone, but not forgotten. These symbols can be called upon, if needed, but only with the blood of a Nepa'Daem. Admon's only other weapons are those that were born to him. In his human form, his only weapons are his razor sharp teeth, built for slashing through the skin of his opponent. In his true form, the large scorpion pinchers and thick tail with poisoned stinger tend to be a force to be reckoned with.

Special Attacks: With Anima'Bacculum there are many special attacks that can be preformed. Each of the thirty symbols turn the staff into a different weapon. For example, the attack known as cuspises, will cause spikes to protrude throughout the length of the staff. Discindo breaks the staff into two, with a long chain between them. The venom of the Nepa'Daem is a special attack that was born to him. It is one of the most poisonous in all the realms. At one time, they were hunted for their venom, their stinger cut off as a trophy and venom sold to the highest bidder. Admon is one of the last of his kind, because of this reason.

Special Defenses: Admon is immune to almost all types of animal venom, because he himself carries very potent venom in his body. He is resistant to disease, unable to contract most viruses. Admon also heals quickly, not so much so that he will heal in front of the naked eye, but a deep wound would take days to heal, instead of weeks. Admon's mind is also resistant to telepath's, he has no telepathic abilities himself, but as the ability to keep his mind shielded from anyone who has this ability.

History: The history of an ancient being is often blurred by time. It is because of this reason that in death and resurrection, Admon began again. Admon Yue Malik died of internal hemorrhage due to Peripherin parasites. These parasites ate away at his nerves and internal structure, until Admon began slowly bleeding out of every orifice, and slowly died an agonizing death in the arms of his only spawn. Navar sealed her father's body in the cave in which he'd lived, leaving him to rest in peace. Years went by and Navar never returned, however Admon's eternal sleep was broken. The tomb of the last full blooded Nepa'Daem was exposed.

Darcie/Revelin/Leila/ Barassah Straight

(CHARACTER PROFILE – CREATION DATE: UNKNOWN)

Full Name: Darcie Straight, Revelin Straight, Leila Straight, and Barassah Straight
Race: Human (Mutated)
Job: Serial Killer
Overview: The quads are human however they can shift between the four personalities in a single body. They can not shift into anything other than the four siblings, which is what separates them and makes them a magical human and not a shape shifter. This is not a racial trait, but a genetic abnormality.
Powers: They have no abilities more than a normal human, however they take multiple personality disorder to a whole other level.
The Straights are very good at what they do. Darcie is the brains, Revelin the heart, Barassah the brute strength, and Leila is the inner child.
Their shift is a physical shift between the four personalities. They were born this way, technically you can't tell the difference between the girls other than Darcie has a scar over her face, while Barassah and Leila do not. Darci's hair tends to have red streaks, as well. The only actual full body shift is when Revelin comes out and only because he is male. All four look quite a bit alike, because they are quadruplets. The idea

for this character came from DID (Dissociative Identity Disorder) or Multiple Personality Disorder. In a fantasy setting, I wanted to take this disorder to another level by allowing the four personalities to actually have their own physical identities as well as mental identities. Four siblings, one body, all four have very different personalities. It takes a few minutes for them to shift, it isn't instantaneous. However one usually has control of the body for a period of time (days, weeks, etc) depending on how long that personality can maintain control. Darcie and Revelin tend to be the stronger minded of the four, therefor they are able to be in control of the body for longer periods of time, but because of the extra energy that their shared brain has serving as a central mind for all four, they do wear out and another identity has to take control. None of them have any special powers, but each of them has their own mental disorder, on top of the obvious. In any case, how did it come about? Their mother was on experimental drugs (and/or potions) to become pregnant, which caused a multiple pregnancy, however the cells did not spilt. It isn't completely apparent what goes on within their body from a genetic standpoint, but it is probable that taken at different times they would have the same blood type, but different DNA, something like a genetic Chimera would have. They can't separate, by magical ways or otherwise, because they would all die, each needs the other to survive. Just like any siblings, they don't all get along which means they tend to seem to talk to themselves quite a bit, but in truth they are talking to the other dormant siblings. Only one can be in control of the body at a time, which means even though they can communicate with each other through the shared mind, the dormant personalities can not themselves communicate with the outside world until they are in control of the body.

Jayne

(CHARACTER PROFILE – CREATION DATE: JULY 2009)

Full Name: Jayne
Race: Enfleshed Doll (Formally a Ragdoll)
Job: Seamstress/Piercer/Tattoo Artist (Needles are her specialty.)
Mind Stat: Untrained – 20
Body Stat: Expert – 11
Magic Stat: Skilled – 14
Gender: Female
Alignment: Neutral with Evil Tendencies
Companion: Jack, The Good Doctor (as she calls him), her creator (Unwillingly)
Marital Status: She was once involved with a marionette, but it didn't work out, his strings were tangled elsewhere.
Hair Color: Greyish Black
Eye Color: Black, like shiny buttons (However, sometimes they glow slightly blue, green, or purple.)
Height: 5'
Weight: 75lbs.
Age: Unknown
Immunities: Immune to poison, cold (can be frozen, but she won't feel it), physical beatings
Weaknesses: Fire
Description: She is filled with stuffing and has no human organs or endowments. She does not bleed.
Carried Items: Two spindles of thread, one package of seven

needles, one tiny pair of scissors, three razor blades, three small packages of matches, and seven gold coins in case she would need more thread

Distinguishing Marks: Evert so often the fine threading of her seams can be seen, however the Good Doctor did well with her reconstruction. The earliest memories Jayne has is of being sewn together, she watched each stitch as the needle was pressed to the skin-like fabric. She was The Creator's first success at life. Her skin had been greyish in tone, made from the tanned flesh of an elf. The skin had no feeling, allowing her to sew herself up if needed in the years to come, however underneath that sewn living flesh she was merely straw and cotton. For years she survived as a ragdoll, five foot in height an atrocity of a creation. She watched silently as The Creator brought new and more perfected creations to life, among those was the small one that must not be named. Jayne had always called her The Light, because not only did the mirror she carried blaze with the brightness of a thousand souls, she was the most prized possession of The Creator. Days turned into months and those months turned into years, years that The Creator ignored her and The Light blossomed into a prime specimen. It was after these many years that Jayne decided to leave her home within the confines of The Creator. The years that followed were strange, there were times when sje lived a happy life, her doll form not much of a bother to her at all, however strange it was to see a living ragdoll. Other days, mostly nights, became dark with...what she soon found was the control of The Creator's sinister plots for her. The black-outs lasted for sometimes minutes, sometimes days, but always she would wake up to be bloody and broken. From the first moment she awoke from one of these, she knew she had to look for a cure. She had no blood from which to bleed, which told her that she was being used against her will for evilness that was not within her to create. In secret, she searched for a powerful mage or doctor to take away the pain of the darkness, until one day she found him. The man appeared in the darkness, the smell of surgery upon him. Jayne never really knew what compelled The Good Doctor to save her, however with weeks of work on his part, Jayne was transformed into the beauty of a living doll that she is today. Her creator's control is no longer, however now she is indebted to the service of another.

Navar Yue Malik

(CHARACTER PROFILE – CREATION DATE: JANUARY 2010)

Full Name: Navar Yue Malik
Race: Half Nepa'Daem/Half Human
Job: Odd Jobs (Professional liar, in many cases.)
Mind Stat: Skilled – 14
Body Stat: Expert – 11
Magic Stat: Untrained – 20
Gender: Female
Age: Looks in her late teens, however is around 12 or 13
Father: Admon Yue Malik (She does not know her mother.)
Siblings: She is her father's only child.
Marital Status: Unattached
Children: None
Alignment: Chaotic Neutral
Loyalties: Only to the purposes of her father.
Height: 5'6"
Weight: 120lbs.
Hair Color: Long, Straight, Pure Red
Eye Color: Ice Blue
Skin Tone: Very Fair
Scars/Tattoos: None Known
History: "Blood of my blood, flesh of my flesh" Navar's creation had always been out of legacy more than want for a child. Her father, Admon Yue Malik, knew that he was dying long before the fits of bloody coughing, he could feel the slow process of his organs slowly starting to shut themselves

down. The egg that was implanted into the human female was created of his own blood and body, acting much like a parasite to the woman, until she eventually gave birth to the baby girl. Navar didn't have even a moment with the woman that was technically her mother. Admon took her quickly, protecting and teaching her, treating her more as a prodigy than a child. She grew rapidly until she looked and had the strengths of a young woman, instead of the pre-teen that her years would have made her. Her father taught her everything that he knew and even though the two had much different sets of abilities, he forced her to strive for her full potential. Unfortunately one large inheritance Navar received from her father was his indifference and arrogance. As she goes through life, her father now passed from that fatal disease, she lives by his teachings...pretending the feelings for life and her father that she has inside do not exist.

Physical Abilities: Accelerated healing, Bone Manipulation, Sonic Scream

Mental Abilities: Omni-linguism (The ability to know any language without learning it), Astral trapping (The ability to trap an astral being, spirit, ghost, etc. into a specific place), Memory manipulation (The ability to erase, enhance, or implant memories), Time Manipulation

Physical Weaknesses: She is not very strong, she has normal human female strength. She is immune to disease, but not poison. Most of her abilities will make her tired if she uses them too frequently.

Mental Weaknesses: Anger, Emotion even though she tries to ignore it, the loss of her father.

Freesia

(CHARACTER PROFILE – CREATION DATE FEBRUARY 2010)

Full Name: Freesia
Alias: Frost/Freeze
Race: Ice Phoenix
Job: None
Mind Stat: Untrained – 20
Body Stat: Novice – 17
Magic Stat: Expert – 11
Marital Status: Perpetually Single
Alignment: Chaotic Evil
Gender: Female
Height: 5'3"
Weight: 97lbs.
Age: 24 years (in this life)
Eye Color: Light Blue
Hair Color: Pure White
Scars/Tattoos: No scars/ She has tribal markings covering the majority of her back, but it's not always visible. When visible, it is a glowing white-blue.
History: Freesia, as she calls herself in this life, does not remember the day that she came into existence, nor the name she was born with, however she does remember how many past lives she has survived through. That number is currently seven. Death is but another beginning, a new beginning that means death once more. This endless cycle of beginnings and ends has begun to tire her in this life. She had become as cold

as the ice she creates. Freesia can be as mild mannered as she is energetic and there really is no pattern to her moods. She tends to do as she pleases, suiting her own purposes above any others. In past lives, her abilities have been put to good use as a nurse, able to freeze wounds closed, a special healing agent in this specific type of ice. However, in her experience people are less than grateful for her assistance. This healing agent, if ingested, can also cleans a person's system, as it does hers. Although, whether she deems one worthy of her help, is always to be seen.

Immunities: Water/Ice Attacks, Infection, Body Alteration (includes any type of race altering bite such as vampire, zombie, werewolf, etc. also includes magic that might penetrate or alter her body).

Defenses: Regeneration/Resurrection (Body/Life Only herself), Frost Heal (Can be used on herself and others)

Abilities: Ice Spikes, Freeze, Frost Touch

Likes/Dislikes: Warmth, Night Time, Sugar, Music/Rain, The Sun, Fire, Spicy Foods

Weaknesses: She doesn't carry any weapons and can be harmed by weapons, because she does not wear armor. Fire attacks, she does burn. Any other human weaknesses that are not listed as an immunity.

Divinity the Incarnate

(CHARACTER PROFILE – CREATION DATE: MARCH 2010)

Full Name: Divinity the Incarnate
Race: Imortali* (Physically human, however with an immortal soul that passes from life to life, see history).
Job: Ward of the Church of Corvosa
Mind Stat: Skilled – 14
Body Stat: Untrained – 20
Magic Stat: Skilled – 14
Marital Status: Single
Enemies: None
Alignment: True Neutral
Gender: Female
Age: 13 (Technically)
Eye Color: Green
Hair Color: Blonde
Skin Type: Fair
Tattoos/Scars: Laced grey tribal here and there on her body
Physical Description: Divinity is, for the most part, a very solemn girl, her expression always holding and empty and almost sad look. She is not one to laugh and only on rare occasion will smile, however when she does it seems to light the room with a warm glow. It often seems as if she is uncaring, however has a generally empathetic nature about her. She is very soft spoken and tends to remain quiet unless she has something important to say.
History: Divinity, named by the Church of Corvosa, upon her

discovery, has been known as Divinity for many lifetimes. Although, the Church of Corvosa does not truly own her, her soul has been under their protection for many generations.
Divinity was born amongst the ancients, human by all accounts, however her race is not defined by their physical characteristics. The Imortali are what they are because their soul is immortal. To Divinity and others like her, a lifetime is but a moment in time. Her soul has seen several bodies, all resembling each other. Paintings in the halls of the church, depict most of her incarnations, each with similar qualities. The religion of the church is not your normal religion, as they truly worship no god, but are dedicated in the service of the Imortali. Very few true Imortali exist, although new souls are at times added under their protection. The physical body of an Imortali is like any other human, fragile and able to be destroyed with ease, however upon death an Imortali is reborn to a new body, inside of a new life. The Church of Corvosa not only protects their wards, but seeks out the rebirth of each Imortali after it's physical death.
Although an Imortali's physical death isn't able to be predicted, often the Imortali will know the family they are going to be reborn to in their next life. When the information is able to be gathered, the Corvosa document it thoroughly and begin to seek out the new pair of humans, assuming they have already been born into this world, and keep track of the pair, without interfering in their natural lives. When the child is born, the reborn Imortali, it is taken from the parents either by monetary means or by physical force, if necessary. Because of the nature of the birth, the physical parents of the child are not allowed to be a part of the Imortali's life for fear

of tainting the knowledge that the Imortali possesses.

All Imortali are born with extensive mental abilities, although they must develop the to their full potential as their new physical brain develops, magical abilities are always specific to each Imortali, and physical skills are almost never encouraged. The nature of the Imortali is soul and mind based, thus the realm of physical knowledge is unimportant. They are, however, taught some basic survival skills, in case they were to be separated from the church. The mind of an Imortali is unable to be penetrated by any means, not only because of the sacred state that they are in, but because it is impossible to break its ancient barriers.

Divinity, herself, is among the oldest surviving Imortali, her soul is so old that even the Corvosa are unable to determine its origins. She has long forgotten most of the more ancient lives that she has possessed, however assumes they are filed deep in her subconscious. Because of the inability to access the information in her mind, the Corvosa have merely been able to document the past lives she is able to remember and the more recent since she has been under their protection.

**Note: The Imortali are unconcerned with death and do not fear it. Often they are known to become obsessed with seeking out physical death, so they are able to start anew. Some ancient Imortali have even become obsessed with 'Final Death', because they have become tired of life.

Skilled Attacks: Telekinesis, Telepathy, Persuasion, Basic Light and Shadow Magic, Basic Elemental Magic

Skilled Defense: Any sort of mental probing and attack is useless, her mind is too complexly patterned to allow any sort of probed communication. The church tends to send a bodyguard with her on occasion, one which has been sworn to protect her, however, she does not always allow the church to watch her every move.

Unique Weaponry: None

Immunities: Disease, Poison, Body Altering Pathogens (Vampire, Werewolf, Zombie, etc.)

Harlow Montgomery-Starr

(CHARACTER PROFILE – CREATION DATE: JULY 2010)

Full Name: Harlow Montgomery-Starr
Race: Human/Rieshan (Four Armed Humanoid)
Job: Entertainer/Waitress at Skid Row (A Members's Only Club)
Mind Stat: Untrained – 20
Body Stat: Expert – 11
Magic Stat: Untrained – 20*
*She has the potential for magic, however knows none for now. She has no known potential for mind based skills.
Overview: All human weaknesses, increased upper body strength due to her extra set of arms.
She has no known immunities or special powers at this time.
She is milk intolerant.
History: Sometimes I like to imagine my young life as nothing more than a dream, a nightmare to be more truthful. A nightmare that I could never wake up from, the scars hidden deep inside, the damage done in the darkness I grew up in. I suppose the best way to start is always from the beginning, not the beginning of my life, but the true beginning of how I came to be. My mother was raised in a socially aristocratic family. High scale parties, private schools, her life was planned out from the day that she was born. Everything changed when she met a girl that made life more exciting, a girl that took her from the confines of her straight and narrow. Unknown to my grandparents, my mother began breaking away

into a life of parties, boys, and alcohol. It was the night of her seventeenth birthday that I was conceived, through the use of a 'roofie colada', a single drink that would forever change her life and bring me into the world. My mother was home schooled from the moment my grandparents learned of the unplanned pregnancy, a punishment that took her away from the world she enjoyed and further chained her to the path that was made to be her life. My grandparents kept my mother from public view when she began to show, telling others that she was merely focusing on her schooling or that she wasn't feeling well. She wasn't allowed to see any friends, only family members and our family doctor. I grew healthy inside her womb during those months and my mother grew fond of me. I was a part of her then, it didn't matter to her who my father was. Every kick she felt, she treasured. However, with every month that went by, my grandparents came closer and closer to their ultimate decision. The day I was born, there wasn't any doubt in their minds. My mother went into labor the 29th of June, it was a beautiful day. The family doctor was called to my grandparents' house, they weren't sure what to expect and to risk the exposure of their pregnant daughter was unimaginable. My mother's labor was long, but in the early morning hours of the next day, I was born, a healthy baby girl…by most standards. As my eyes opened on the world for the first time and I took my first breath, I let out a healthy cry. I threw my arms out, startled…all four of them. The doctor's surprise was apparent, as for a moment, he paused. However, handed me to the nurse to bathe, weigh, and measure. The nurse merely smiled down at me with soft eyes. As the doctor cleaned himself up, he watched me closely, thinking on what he would tell my grandparents when they entered the room. I was wrapped in a blanket and handed gently to my young mother, looking up at her with dark eyes, now quiet with wonder about my new world. My mother watched me in awe and curiosity, gently running her fingers across my soft, newborn skin. The love in her eyes made me feel safe, her arms warm around me. I fell asleep that day in her arms, ten fingers tangled in her hair. My grandparents, as expected, were appalled and outrage at the birth of their healthy four-armed grandchild. My mother was sent to boarding school immediately, her recovery to be done within the school infirmary. I wouldn't see her again until I was eight years old. I don't remember much about my early life, the nurse that helped with my birth was paid to become a full-time nanny. My grandparents hardly acknowledged that I existed. My nanny, Tressa, was responsible for all of my care. She was given a credit card and with it there was no limits. Nan-Tress, as I had called her, loved me as her own child. She, herself, had grown up in a world of oddities, in the know about magical creatures and she had told me stories of a world hidden amongst out own. It wasn't until I was five years old that my grandparents began to introduce me to society, for short periods of time. Nan-Tress had made a special a special harness for my lower set of arms, it hid all signs of the offensive limbs, but created an image of an 'overly healthy' child. I remember how uncomfortable it was to have the arms tethered to me, the pins and needles that came as they fell asleep in the harness. I never truly liked it, but the laws of society said that in public, I had to, as Nan-Tress said, 'hide how special' I was. On my eighth birthday, my mother came home for the summer and through much protest from my grandparents, I wasn't forced to wear the harness. I will always remember that summer as the best summer of my life, but it was also the worst. My mother loved me, she didn't care that I was different, she loved me for who I was. At the end of the summer, I lost her. On August 20th, she pulled out into a busy intersection, and was hit by an oncoming SUV. She died the next day from critical injuries. When my mother died, I was further forgotten by my grandparents. The social outings stopped and I was placed in a school for the 'gifted'. Nan-Tress had arranged for me to go to a school for magical kids and even though I had no magic of my own, I fit in well. While I was gone, I wrote to her every day, as I still do. I graduated from high school with honors, but in my grandparents eyes, their job was finished. I was sent out into the world on my own, without more than a couple of thousand dollars. Since then, I have had several jobs, several men in my life, including the recent Mr. Starr. While he enjoyed his marriage to me, he enjoyed his nightlife even more. We divorced a year later, due to irreconcilable differences, however are still on decent terms. I kept his name, rather than just the name of my family. I felt as if I had received more love from him in that single year than I had in my entire life before they cast me out into the world. Maybe someday I will find someone to connect with, but that day is likely not today.

Iraciella the Red

(CHARACTER PROFILE – CREATION DATE: SEPTEMBER 2010)

Full Name: Iraciella the Red
Race: Vampire
Mind Stat: Master – 8
Body Stat: Expert – 11
Magic Stat: Untrained – 20
Overview: Iraciella is one of the oldest vampires existing. She is the basis of the well-known fairy tale of Red Riding Hood. She was created thousands of years ago, when the world was young and when she too was very young. Her physical appearance is not more than 15, but her age in years makes her a vert powerful vampire force. Through the years she has taken werewolf protectors, because of her small form, which has only been able to develop at a skilled level for a vampire. A single werewolf family line has been her protectors for generations, using mind control and the use of her powerful blood as an incentive. She brands her wolves with the symbol for 'Red' on their neck, letting all know that they are under her protection and control. She is well known, but a hidden vampire secret. She is very influential on the vampire council and is the unknown president of the ASPS, her werewolf guard, Raphael St. James poses as a decoy president for the company.

It is because of her child like appearance and her relationship with this werewolf family line that the fairy tale of Red

Riding Hood was created, although it was twisted over the years into something that made her out to be something she wasn't. It suits her, because the appeal of Red Riding Good as a blood stained child wasn't quite so pleasant.

Jimmy Allero

(CHARACTER PROFILE – CREATION DATE: NOVEMBER 2010)

First Name of Character: James Ryan
Last Name or Title: Allero
Aliases: St. Jimmy; The Peacemaker
Race: True Human (Non-Magical)
Job: Leader of the Immunization Society
Alliances: The Immunization Society
Personality: Paranoid; Erratic; Defensive
Likes: Budweiser; Barettas; Cadillacs; Fine Females
Dislikes: Magical Beings; Authority; Cops; Jail
Wrap Sheet: 8 Counts Public Disturbance; 13 Counts Assault; 5 Counts Vandalism; 4 Counts Public Intoxication; 2 Counts Driving While Intoxicated
Body: 11
Magic: 20
Mechanics: 14
Intuitive Aptitude: 11
Gender: Male
Age: 26 years
Height: 6'2"
Weight: 140lbs.
Eye Color: Blue
Hair Color: Brown
Scars: A Few
Tattoos: Many
Piercings: Many

Description: Assailant is covered with tattoos, usually having a full mohawk. He is of a thin, muscular body type. He tends to wear jeans and a t-shirt with steel toed combat boots. He tends to drive a black Cadillac with chrome trim. Suspect is presumed to be armed and dangerous.

Overview: Jimmy has no magical qualities whatsoever, he has every physical human weakness, but he also has quite a bit of alliances. These alliances can get him everything from black market guns and ammunition to back stage concert tickets. His own rage and vengeance toward the world around him tends to be his greatest weapon. (He doesn't have any special abilities at all, he just has an extreme hatred for magical beings.)

"Through trials and tribulations we have come, trudging through this the hour of darkness. With these hands and our God given strength, we shall overcome! We are society, and we are the people of this nation. Rise against, my defenders! My keepers of all that is pure in this world! We will rid ourselves of those who stain it with their mere existence! Our society needs to be immunized of their virus, the blood purified...we are the needle of justice, may our vaccine spread throughout the world!

"As God is my witness, the infidels are going to pay! I am the Spirit of Vengeance, I am and the Peacemaker, I am Saint Jimmy."

Growing up on a small island, magic surrounded James from birth. He was schooled with the werewolf cubs and creatures of all different races and cultures. One of his closest companions was his cousin Harlow, a four-armed humanoid with a spunky personality. However, that all changed when he was fifteen years old and a rogue werewolf pack decided to vacation on the island.

The rogue pack destroyed homes and families, tearing through everything in their wake. Both of James's parents and many other human citizens of the island were killed defending their homes, families, and their friends.

Young James, instead of mourning the loss of his parents, started on a quest of vengeance, directing his rage toward those he felt responsible. In his mind, an island full of magical beings could have prevented his loss and carried out what he felt was justice against the pack. The rogue pack was incarcerated; however, the death penalty was not decided to be given to them.

James left the island at fifteen, beginning to gather an army against those who had done him wrong. Not just the pack that had killed his parents, but those who refused to protect them and carry out justice.

Leaving all of his past behind him, except for his own hatred for magical beings, he now calls himself Saint Jimmy. He lives in a fairly large city, running a group of rebels that he calls The Immunization Society.

Harvey J. Blythe

(CHARACTER PROFILE – CREATION DATE FEBRUARY 2011)

Character First Name: Harvey J.
Character Last Name or Title: Blythe
Race: Vampire (human)
Job: Musician
Mind Stat: Novice - 17
Body Stat: Expert - 11
Magic Stat: Untrained - 20
Title: Laggard
Alignment: True Neutral
Mate: None
Occupation: Musician
Race: Vampire (Human)
Age: 26 Years (Eternally)
Height: 6.0
Weight: 147lbs.
Hair Color: Dirty Blonde
Eye Color: Blue
Description: Harvey J. is a small framed man, thin and not imposingly tall. His
blonde hair shags around his face, his chin always covered in a light scruff. He tends to wear clothing of simple means, whatever ends up on his person seems to be his clothing of choice. He tends to wear thick brown leather, steel toed boots, worn from years of constant 'usage'.
Harvey J. isn't much of a fighter, in fact, he tends to stay out

of anything
that requires much physical activity on his part. He likes to read and is quite the musician. He smokes, he drinks, he considers himself the best of what the Blythe family has to offer. He grew up with a large family, his sister, born directly after him, tended to be his closest companion. His youth and young adult years were spent trying to find a way out of doing as many things as possible, pitting siblings against each other and working together when situations called for it. At the age of 20, after a long night of drinking, he was hitched to a woman twice his age.

Assuming the situation would get him away from the life of the middle child, he stuck with the marriage for a while...until a week later. Technically he's still married to Regina, however he refuses to see her again. Don't ask him about it.

Powers: Basic vampire abilities and weaknesses. No magic, he doesn't shapeshift. He's a scrapper, just using weapons he finds. (i.e. broken bottles, chairs, etc.) Although, he's really not much of a fighter.

Bellamy Buchanan

(CHARACTER PROFILE – CREATION DATE: APRIL 2015)

Full Name: Bellamy Vincent Buchanan
Alias: Dead Shot
Home State: Texas/Oklahoma Area
Race: Touched Human
Age: 26 years
Description: He is not a redneck or cowboy, he is a survivalist with a concealed carry permit. He always carries his black and silver Ruger LC9.
History: After his mother died from an intruder when he was 14, he was raised by his father who was not home much, they lived out in the country, learning magical power, and practiced shooting. He has the magical power of metal working. He can bend, shift manipulate any type of metal with magic, doesn't use unless needed which makes his aim with a bullet dead on. He hates crime, but would never be a cop, he does not like how the law works. His dad passed away within the last few years. He moved to New Orleans because it seemed like a fun place to be. He has a small apartment above a Chinese food place, somehow he always smells like Chinese food, no matter how hard he tries. He does not wear much cologne. He now owns an arsenal of weapons…left to him when his father passed away. He no longer has any living relatives. He has a Husky named pistol.
History: Bellamy's history as the man he is now, truly began when his life was set down his current path. When

Bellamy was 14 years old, his mother, the scientist, Dr. Laura Buchanan, was killed and her lab burned to the ground. Investigators deemed it a random attack, but Bellamy had other suspicions. The next couple of years he poured himself into his own investigation, trying to get the authorities to listen to his theories and what he had found, however no one would listen to the young man. They considered him grief stricken and later paranoid over the loss of his mother, trying to get him to take medication and once even committing him, because of his 'crazy' ideas. However, Bell's ideas were not so crazy after all.

These tragic events somehow triggered something inside of him to come to the surface, like alight switch being switched on, and Bell slowly learned he could bend and contort metal to his will. Since this realization, Bellamy has trained himself in hand to hand combat, his magical ability, and multiple different weapons, making it his mission to not only avenge his mother's death, but to destroy the secret organization that killed her.

New Salem

(FANTASY LOCATION PROFILE – CREATION DATE: DECEMBER 2014)

Alternate Name: New Salem City
Government: Democracy
Leader: The Magical Council (Current Leader of Processions, Haliese Rebecca Herrick- Bishop)
Primary Races: Magical Races mostly (Non-magical races allowed by application only)
Climate: Underground, simulated sky and climate Resources: All New England Resources
Dangers: Vigilantes, Rebels, criminals, etc. (Also some magical creatures that have been exposed to the underground for sanctuary.)
New Salem City Historical Archives: The History of New Salem City, in truth, is largely the history of the House of Herrick. To understand why it was founded and how it was created, a person would have to understand the history of the Herrick family, their origins, and their way of life. Truly, it was a threat to that way of life that influenced their decision to move underground, along with family, friends, and others that were accustomed to a mythical, magical way of their own. This is the story of New Salem...this is the story of the beginning of a new civilization.
Henry John Herrick, fifth son of Sir William Herrick of Leicester, London, and Beaumont Park, was born in the year of 1606. He grew up in Beau Manor, Longhborough Parish,

Co of Leicester, England. Henry, much as his father, was born an old-world witch. Practicing in the arts of magic from a young age and excelling, as did his brethren and ancestors before him. A pure line of magic stemming back from Ancient times, times before documentation. However, in the era Henry was born, magic was much as it is today, a mostly hidden from the rest of the world. In England during these times, races were separate, hidden even from each other. To Henry, no other world existed. Their line had always been upper class, never wanting for anything and passing down a rich heritage and monetary wealth. It was this wealth that allowed Henry to cross the ocean to seek his destiny in the New World, settling in the colony of Salem in the year 1629. Henry found that the rise of the New World meant many things to a man of magic, new sights, new experiences, and most of all new people. It was soon after he reached the colonies that he discovered the existence of the many different races within the magical world. Most were refugees traveling in the guise of religious freedom, when truly, they were looking for racial freedoms and the ability to live their way of life without societal secrecies. These races were able to mingle in this new country, functioning as a society within a society, without allowing humans the knowledge of their existence. It had been decided early on humans, with their limited capabilities to understand and accept the world of magic, would be kept without knowledge of the truth of the world they lived in by the Magical Council. The Magical Council was formed, not as a governing entity, but as structure creators and enforcers by which their self-governed society could conduct great decisions. Henry Herrick was this council's first Leader of Processions or LP. Within the years that followed this structure proved positive. Humans and magical beings were able to coexist as if there were no differences, the people were at peace. That was until the year of 1691, when an accidental exposure led to years of prosecution and pain for both sides. Henry Herrick, being of influential stature within the community, was able to secure himself a position on the jury for the witch trials of Salem. Many of the other council members and magical citizens were able to also keep themselves out of harm's way by gaining positions of enforcement and inconspicuous nature. However, many were not so lucky. As it seemed to the members of the magical community, these ravenous humans had no way of distinguishing magical beings from their own kind, which caused their own race to also lose many, many citizens. These were dark times for Salem, times of confusion and chaos, but also the messenger of a valuable lesson and the savior of the magical people of Salem. In the year 1755, Amos Herrick was born. The trials had mostly died down and he was able to live a childhood of normalcy, though his gifts remained in secret as they had in the generations before. The magical races, though they knew of each other, no longer mingled between themselves, for fear of being discovered. It was Amos Herrick, in his young adulthood, that discovered a way to bring their world together once more. At the age of twenty years old, Amos began working on the secret underground city of New Salem. He, along with a few other influential families built the city from the ground up and within 7 years, their masterpiece was finished. In the year of 1782, a strange plague made its way through the city of Salem,

Massachusetts, taking with it many, many family lines. The 'deaths' of these families on the surface, allowed a peaceful passage of these families to the underground city and a deliverance into a life of their choosing. Since the year of founding in 1782 to current, New Salem City has grown exponentially, expanding underground as needed and largely outnumbering its sister city's population. New Salem City is a Mecca for magical races, a place they can live in peace without threat of exposure or prosecution for their mere existence. As long as the laws of the city are followed, all those of 'Knowing' are allowed, including non-magical humans. Measures are taken to ensure the longevity of the city, but for over two centuries, the people of New Salem City have flourished.

Other Notes: Entrance to New Salem City can only be accessed through teleportation or magically sealed staircases. These staircases are guarded by NSPD and the admission policies are carefully enforced. Teleportation is monitored in and out of the city as well. True Humans are not allowed in or out without a magical passport. Passports can be gained through a process of careful evaluation on the surface by the Magical Council. The leading government of New Salem City is much like most governments, however, is governed by the city's Magical Council, decided on by democratic vote. This Council is governed by the laws of The Veiland those who enforce them. They also work closely with governing forces from other magical cities and communities. Current LP position belongs to the oldest surviving member of the Herrick Household, Haliese Rebecca Herrick- Bishop (1894 - Current; 120 yrs), passed down to her by her father, Ketterick Richard Herrick. Ketterick Herrick was the only surviving son of Amos Herrick after his elder brother, Lucian Henry Herrick's death in 1925. LP has been and will be passed on to the oldest living member of the family furthermore, as decreed by city and council mandate. This position is the only position on the council that remains an involuntary position, because of the origins of the House of Herrick and founding of the city, all others are democratically voted upon by the city itself coinciding with general elections of city, state, and federal U.S. governments.

New Salem City Declaration of Decision

By Decision, September 7th, 1782.

The unanimous Declaration of the thirteen Magical Council members of the city of New Salem, Massachusetts,

When in the Course of events, it becomes necessary for one people to dissolve the bonds which have connected them with another classification of peoples, and to assume among the powers of the earth, the separate and equal station to which the Laws of Nature entitle them, a decent respect to the opinions that require they should declare the causes which impel them to the separation.

These laws, being necessary for a peaceful society, with respect to racial differences and infringement upon those the rights of others, shall not be violated and ignored. Above all others governmental, religious, natural, and supernatural, these laws of the City of New Salem are placed forth and accessible publicly to all within the city and shall be posted about the city as such.

I. No person shall be allowed to knowingly harm another, even if it be by

religious or racial purpose. Penalties shall be imposed upon those who do so, having received proper notification by way of this declaration.

II. Any willful destruction of the property of another or that of the city of New Salem without prior permission will not be tolerated and shall be penalized accordingly by decision of trial by council.

III. No single person may take the property of another, all land and possessions must be purchased or given freely.

IV. No governing official may assume control, nor pass on their position, with exception of the Leader of Processions, which shall always remain within the lineage of the founder of New Salem, Amos Herrick.

V. Willful harassment of another creature or persons, by any reason not pertaining to the enforcement of law, shall not be tolerated.

VI. The City of New Salem shall accept any creature or persons of any race, gender, magical denomination, or lifestyle and not discriminated against any single person or creature for any reason based on attributes born to them. However, knowledge of New Salem and it's society is to be limited to those of magical orientation or those accepted into this knowledge by the Magical Council of New Salem. These allowed, non-magical persons and creatures and to carry an allowance passport at all times within the city of New Salem and will produce this passport upon request of a proven city official of New Salem.

VII. In order to maintain separation from that of the city of Old Salem, all entry points to the city will not only be magically barred, but also guarded at all times by officers deemed appropriate by the council of the city of New Salem.

Teleportation, while allowable, will be highly monitored to ensure proper security of the city itself.
VII. Traveling between dimensions within the city, much as barred by world magical law, is strictly prohibited.
IX. Those persons or creatures found to be over the power cap for major cities, will not be allowed to enter, unless designated by the council beforehand.
X. The City of New Salem and its council shall not infringe upon the rights of its citizens, allowing all to live life as they choose without fear of prosecution or judgment of any natural born abilities or qualities. New Salem shall never, within fair limits, require its citizens to hide any attributes that deem them different from any other race or people.

Robert Ketterick 'R.K.' Bishop

(CHARACTER PROFILE – CREATION DATE: 2014)

Full Name: Robert Ketterick Bishop
Alias: R.K.
Race: Human (Old-World Witch – Not Wiccan)
Age: Adult (26-39 yrs)
Job: Heir to the Herrick line
Mind: Novice – 17
Body: Expert – 11
Magic: 17 – Novice
Overview: R.K. is from a very old, very rich family line and has been trained thoroughly in the art of self-defense. He is skilled in fencing, hand to hand combat, small weapons, and a skilled marksman with a rifle, handgun, and a bow. However, R.K. does not carry any weapons on him he prefers to use his head and the weapons the world provides for him.
Personality: R.K. is an easy going guy, for the most part, a bit excitable, slightly obsessive about certain things, and careless about others. He likes to go his own way with things, often not conforming to rules, but not truly breaking them either. He does not like authority figures much, but respects the person behind the authority. He's very social in general, but at times can be reclusive, as well, sometimes it can merely depend on his mood what his personality is like.
Strengths: Wealth, friends, family

Weaknesses: A pretty face, beer, adrenaline fueled activities

History: R.K. comes from a very long lineage that can be traced back to the very beginning of the city of Salem, Massachusetts when his (many greats) grandfather came from England to the Americas. Personally, R.K. was raised by his parents, Hartford and Shelly Bishop, under the line of Ketterick Herrick, of the Herrick Household. R.K. comes from old money and is heir to Bishop Enterprises, however chooses not to take on his father's business, owning a night club and a member of a band.

Sylk de Azazeyl

(CHARACTER PROFILE – CREATION DATE: JANUARY 2016)

Full Name: Sylk de Azazeyl
Race: Half Lillu Demon/Half Gregori**
Age: Very Old (85 yrs & older)
Job: Seductress/Betrayer/Mistress of Deception
Mind Stat: Untrained – 20
Body Stat: Skilled – 14
Magic Stat: Skilled – 14
Overview: Sylk is a child of the Abyss, born to the darkness and parents with cold, dark hearts. Sylk, being half Lillu Demon ad half Gregori was cursed from birth, damned to either the Abyss or Hell. However, sometimes there are benefits to a cursed existence. Sylk, not only received her parents' curses, but their abilities and beauty, as well. Angelic of face and demeanor, Sylk is often a wolf in sheep's clothing. From her long rose-colored hair to her deep cerulean eyes, to her slender curvaceous form, to her long and shapely legs, she is the pinnacle of humanoid perfection. Her movements consistently display a predatory grace, every step meaningful and planned, down to the flitter of an eyelash. Her scent of rich sweets flows from her in abundance, of cakes and cookies, sugar candies, gingerbread, and pastries, all wrapped into one but yet none, a scent few others possess. Her touch is gentle, skin as soft as a feather, pale porcelain and warm like the tender lick of a flame. Cold, calculating deceiver, watcher. Sylk takes pleasure in watching the suffering of others, more

than doing so herself. She is more likely to order or force others to cause death and destruction for her and take enjoyment from viewing pain and torture. Though she doesn't like to get her hands dirty often, she can and will do what she wishes or needs to get what she wants.

(**Note: For the purposes of this character, I modified the race. Gregori, although they have similarities to celestial beings are actually a race dwelling in the depths, whether it be Hell or the Abyss. Because they appear so similar to celestial beings, there are legends about the race having been from the heavens and descended into Hell, however there is no definite evidence that the Gregori have ever dwelled anywhere but the depths. The physical appearance of the Gregori is not much different than that of a celestial, however there are a few large differences between the two. The wings of the Gregori are dark, like that of a raven, black with the shine of blue or green tones. Full blooded Gregori generally have dark hair and blue or green eyes. Gregori are most generally evil with lawful or chaotic tendencies. They can be neutral, however never good in alignment. A Gregori's power nearly mirrors that of a celestial, using unholy magic as a basis for their skills and abilities. The Gregori are a very intelligent race and are often influences of many happenings in Hell and on the mortal plane. Though they cannot travel outside the plane of Hell, they are able to overtake the mind of lesser creatures and humanoids, the possession allowing them to communicate with the world above. Azazeyl, Sylk's father, is full blooded Gregori and adviser to the Prince of the Second Plane of the Abyss. Because Sylk is only half Gregori, she does not have wings like her father, she has the sharp teeth claw-like nails, and her eyes, though slit like a cat's, much like her mother's are, cerulean with a slight glow to them that allows her to see in the dark/low light.

Combat Abilities:

Aura Absorption – The ability to absorb another's aura to gain the power of their life essence, whether it be to gain their powers or merely just their life force. The ability to use the aura can be temporary or permanent, depending on what is absorbed.

Curse Induction – Allows Sylk to induce a curse upon the living, dead, or undead, by attaching a spell to their essence.

'Word of Chaos' – Basically the ability of Murphy's Law, whatever could go wrong, will go wrong. The ability to cause the worst possible scenario to be the only option.

Non-Combat Abilities:

Astral Projection – The ability to project her soul away from her own body, so as to travel long distances or unseen by the naked eye. Sylk has the ability to choose whether or not she would like to be seen or not in this form, only those with truesight are able to see her if she chooses to remain hidden. With this ability, she is able to inflict temporary possession. While projecting herself away from her body she is able to temporarily possess the body of another person or creature, in order to see what they see, hear what they hear, feel what they feel. She cannot force them to do anything against their will, however that person or creature will not remember anything that happened while possessed, they will simply lose that amount of time, as if it never happened.

Divination – The ability to communicate with the dead. This includes all forms of the dad, including but not limited to:

ghosts, zombies, ghouls, mummies, etc.

Pain Suppression – This ability, stemming from her Gregori blood, can be used on herself and others. It is a useful tool, not only to aide in healing and restoration, but also torture. If pain is maintained to a certain threshold, the body does not go into shock, which allows the body to feel a certain level of pain for the maximum amount of time before physical death.

Dispel Magic – The ability to break magical ties, curses, or spells upon a person, place, and/or thing. Included with this is the gift of truesight, which allows her to see through illusions, invisibility, and anything magically hidden.

Cure Moderate Wounds – The ability to cure wounds of herself and others, as long as they are not fatal. (This ability does not include regeneration of lost or destroyed body parts. This ability is also linked to her blood, which means that she can not touch someone to heal them, her blood must come into contact with the wound or be ingested by the injured or ill.)

Other General Abilities:

Resistances include, but are not limited to: Sickness, mental manipulation, cold, petrification, acid, fire and electricity (lightning).

Dark/low Light Vision

Quick Healing (This ability does not include regeneration of lost or destroyed body parts.)

Resurrection – If Sylk's physical body is killed or destroyed, her soul is send back to the abyss. From there, her body can slowly be regenerated, however this process does time and quite a bit of energy from her soul. There is also the matter of escaping the abyss once more, which is never an easy task. (If Sylk's physical form is destroyed or killed, her skills return to her base stats of 20/14/14, no matter how powerful she has become before she regenerated.) Because she is only half Lillu Demon, she does not have weakness of Truename, knowing her given name yields no power over her.

Weaknesses: Holy Magic/Magical Assistance of the Gods, Blessed Steel

Archibald 'Archie' Kavanaugh

(CHARACTER PROFILE – CREATION DATE: JULY 2016)

Full Name: Archibald 'Archie' Kavanaugh
Race: Human
Age: Young Adult (18-25 years old)
Job: Previously a railroad switchman, now works odd jobs in Pistol Creek
Intelligence: Untrained – 20
Body: Skilled – 14
Aim: Skilled – 14
Description: Archie is a middle aged man at twenty-three years old, considering the life expectancy of the Wild West. He has shoulder length brown hair, often times with a mustache and a bit of scruff framing his jawline. He isn't overly tall, at just above six foot and considering his line of work, tends to be fairly physically fit. Archie tends to be fairly quiet, never having much to say, however that is largely due to his very obvious Irish accent. He doesn't carry much with him, merely a small satchel and an old Irish rifle, leftovers from another life.
History:
Archie was born in Ireland in, the year of our Lord, 1886. His family, he tells little of, not truly liking to relive that time of his life, the time before immigrating to America, the land of opportunity, the land where dreams come true and gold

flows through the veins of every mountain and stream. However, once he arrived, he realized the truth is always truly in the eye of the beholder.

Archie has sold everything in Ireland that he'd had of value, in most part, except for the purchase of the sea voyage and the stage ride to the famous California hills of gold took almost very penny he had, having the assumption many before him also had, that he'd arrive in California and have the ability to merely scoop up handfuls of gold. Unfortunately, that was not the case. Archie, in fact, was a terrible gold miner. This due partly to the act that Archie hadn't the patience for it, nor the temperament. It wasn't long before Archie, broke and beginning to lose hope, signed a contract with the railroad, traveling to the mid-west, where the rail lines were blooming from town to town, hauling the riches of the country to both the east and the west. Months went by and Archie almost worked himself to death, breaking his back for little to no pay.

One evening, while washing himself and his sweat soaked shirt in a river by the light of the moon, he caught a glimpse of his reflection in the water. Within the two years he'd been in this country, it almost seemed to have aged him much more beyond that. His dress shirt that had cost him half of what he made in a week working on the rails, he'd bought in Dublin just before he'd began his new life in America, now tattered, torn, and stained with American soil. To this country, the sound of his voice made him not much better than the dirt, the accent classified his worth in this country. Archie's father had been a physician, his mother a schoolteacher, his family on both sides had been wealthy enough to send both of his parents to Queen Anne's newly built University of Ireland. Archie remembered his mother telling him tales of their romance, the way they knew they had been meant for each other from the moment they met.

He is very intelligent, both of his parents having been to college in Ireland. He has no formal education over small town grade school, except for his mother's teachings, the many books he has read, and assisting his father as a general practice physician. He is very skilled in shooting a rifle, as he and his father were avid hunters in Ireland, as a boy, and he enjoyed target shooting for enjoyment. He is also fairly physically fit from working for the railroad for two years. He has only been in America for around three years now, his main weakness is that when he speaks, at times, he can not conceal his Irish accent. During this time period, Irish workers are not looked at in very high regard. At this point in the U.S., most are ignorant and untrained, and are often times sent to do the worst, most dangerous jobs.

Drake Byrne

(CHARACTER PROFILE – CREATION DATE: OCTOBER 2016)

Full Name: Drake Byrne
Race: Half Demon
Age: Adult (Ages 26 to 39)
Job: Con-artist, but currently leeching off of his sister
Mind Stat: Untrained – 20
Body Stat: Expert – 11
Magic Stat: Untrained – 20
Aliases: Black Byrne, Demon Drake, Dark Drake, Deadly Drake, Son of a Bitch, Asshole (On average, just about any insult that can be given, but it's never bothered him.)
Gender: Male
Hair Color: Dark Brown to Black
Eye Color: Aqua Blue
Height: 6'2"
Weight: 160lbs.
Tattoos/Scars: A few scattered tattoos/ A few scars
Marital Status: Habitually and deservingly single
Children: Of course not, he doesn't want anything to do with the disgusting little creatures
Alignment: Chaotic Evil
Companions: Prefers to be alone
Steed: He doesn't like riding, but he will if he has to
Allies: Only his sister, currently, but they have a love/hate relationship
Enemies: Likely he's made quite a few over the years

Family: Arachne Desirae [Half-Sister, the demon half]
Other Information:
Class: Drake has very little usually.
Personality: Humorous, Flirty, Haughty, Personable, Charming
Likes: Drake likes a good time, a fine wine, a jingle in his pocket, and a beautiful woman at his side.
Dislikes: He dislikes city guards, tattle tales, whistle blowers, trolls [of many different meanings], hot beer, vegetables, many numerous other things.
Strengths and Weaknesses: He has many different strengths and weaknesses. However, on majority his wit/intelligence, his venom, his charm/pheromones, and his quick healing are his strengths. While his weaknesses, include the fact that he likes to drink, he tends to be a bit of a playboy, and he often says many things that he shouldn't. Drake can also have a bit of a temper and can be sometimes easily offended, he will also pick fights with others, even if he's not sure if he can win.
History:
Drake was raised much the same way Arachne had been, by adoptive parents other than his own, because his demon mother tossed him away into the wilds for taking after his human father. However, he was raised mainly at sea. His adoptive father was a pirate by trade and his adoptive mother had been a harlot before she had settled down to the life of a pirate's wife. It hadn't mattered to the couple that Drake was something other than human, merely happy to have a child of their own, as his adoptive mother had contracted a disease that had destroyed her womb, not allowing her to conceive their own child. While Drake was young, his feet

barely touched dry ground, living most of his life at sea with his family and it wasn't until he was an adolescent. It was when he had lost his baby teeth that the venomous sets of fangs grew in and he noticed differences between him and his parents. As a young teen he began to be curious of his real family and began to try and find them. It was while Arachne had been away from Elysium Manor that his quest had led him to her doorstep. Not that the manor was in incredibly good condition, he could tell that though she wasn't there at the time, she would return and he would convince her then that she needed to accept her half brother into her open arms and take care of him, like all older sisters should. This was what he'd planned anyway.

Weapons: Drake is fairly good with venom coated throwing knives, which he keeps a flat bundled set in each boot, easily accessible to him. He also tends to be able to fight fairly well with just about anything he can get his hands on, from a broken bottle to a bar-stool. He's had plenty of practice over the years, having gotten himself into and out of many fights over his life. His adoptive father taught him not only to use the throwing knives, but how to fight, in case he had need of it.

Armor: He tends to wear a mithril chain-mail underneath his shirt most of the time, just so his internal organs are protected. He can heal from most wounds fairly quickly, but a fatal wound is easily attained if one tries hard enough, he is far from immortal.

Special Defenses: Venom. Unlike his sister, his kiss is not poisonous, much like his mother the Black Widow Demon, only his bite can inject venom into his prey. He has a double set of razor sharp, extended canines on either side of his teeth with venom pockets above them that cause such an accursed bite. He has learned how to 'milk' the venom from himself, to coat weapons like his throwing knives with it. His venom is natural, much like a spider bite, not at all like man-made poison, so even those resistant to poison most of the time are not resistant to his venom.

Magic: He has the ability, but not quite the one to actually study such things, he hasn't the patience for it.

Psionics: Also a possibility for his race, but he never much wanted anything to do with mind control, he has pheromones just like his sister that work well enough.

Special Abilities

Pheromones – Love/lust ability, not quite as advanced as his sister's abilities, but he is fairly practiced with controlling when he allows his body to give off the secretions. The pheromones, much as his sister's work on both men and women, compelling them to feel either love or lust for him, at his will. This is a false sensation, but while under the spell of the pheromones, one will feel as if it is real. This ability uses the body stat, as it is a natural ability of the Spider Demon's body.

Venomous Spit – Drake can also spit venom, much like his sister the process is merely a bit different for him to do so [All venom abilities also use his body stat, because they are also a product of his body and not mental or magical abilities.]

Quick Healing – Like Arachne, the demon blood within his body heals him quickly, though any fatal blows can and will kill him. Neither he, nor his sister can regenerate limbs or the sort and they will scar from a holy weapon, because of the blood of the damned.

Tsula 'Bek' Bekehren Hurmuž

(CHARACTER PROFILE – CREATION DATE: JANUARY 2017)

Full Name: Tsula 'Bek' Bekehren Hurmuž
Race: Můra Muž (Moth Man – Mythic)
Age: Young Adult (As a human would appear between 18 to 25)
Occupation: 'Man of the Night'/Cage Fighter
Mind Stat: Untrained – 20
Body Stat: Skilled – 14
Magic Stat: Skilled 14
Description, Bek is an abrasive and bold sort of young man, he tends to rarely wear a shirt, feeling more comfortable in as little clothing as possible. He normally wears very worn pants, with several holes in them, making them as airy as possible for him. Due to his nature, the cold nor the heat bothers him. Often times he is bruised because of his 'second job', however this does not make him less attractive to potential customers, if anything it adds to his allure, as a rugged sort of 'bad boy' type. The young man's movements are fluid and even his fighting style is almost something of a seductive dance. However, he is no devil or demon, his race is rare and he isn't likely to explain it, as he's not even sure of his own potential or capabilities, whereas he grew up and orphan, having left the orphanage as soon as he was able to make his own way in the world. Though his occupations are not the

most savory within the city, Bek is a loyal and trustworthy individual. He might be a bit rough around the edges, but he is far from evil or chaotic. He is not quite lawful, but he does try to keep himself within his own set of internal morals and values. Bek has the potential for greatness, if he can find it.

Physical Abilities: Bek is a street fighter. He's had no formal training, though is more physically inclined than most, his endurance and stamina are a force to be reckoned with. He's not always the most strong fighter fighter in the ring, but often wins many of his fights out of pure stubbornness. He will fight dirty if he has to and uses anything he possibly can to his advantage. His intelligence is apparent however, by the quick witted, strategic moves that he makes. [Bek also has other physical abilities that are unknown to most. He does not share all of his racial traits with the public.]

Magical Abilities: Bek's magical abilities are still developing, as he has had no one to truly teach him the abilities he was born with, but has only figured some out on his own through trial and error. Bek is a powerful seer by nature, born to him as a racial gift.

+Divination – This power not only includes foretelling the future, but contacting the spirits of the dead. With this power he not only is able to speak to ethereal and spiritual beings, but he can sometimes influence them to contact or watch others of his choosing. This allows him to see and watch things that he might not be able to in physical form. However, to be able to see the future of specific persons, for now, he must physically touch them. Bek does not always have great control of this ability and will sometimes accidentally see things he shouldn't see, however normally when this

happens, it is not a good prediction and is forced on him.
+Light Magic – Bek can use light as a force of combat, not only to blind opponents, but as an energy source. He can use either hot or cold light, with a spectrum of colors that tend to correspond with that which he attacks with. This ability comes from spiritual magic, though he knows nothing of any Gods and is loyal to none that exist beyond his current plane of existence. His magic is derived and attached to his soul. It is unknown if he could use these powers beyond his physical form. When hit with this particular attack, an opponent feels almost as if they were hit by a brick wall, it is a very powerful blow when in full force.
+Astral Projection (undeveloped) – This is an ability that, while Bek knows he has the potential for, he has not been able to develop it. He has only projected his spiritual form a handful of times accidentally and is unable to control this ability. He has tried many times to do so intentionally, however none have been successful.
[Bek is capable of much more, however is undeveloped in numerous abilities as of right now.]

The Arrival

(LARGE SCALE GAME: BEGINNING POST [UNPLAYED] - 2016 – THE TALE OF SORIN/MARRIS/STERLING)

Sorin looked at the piece of crumbling parchment, as he unwrapped the new book from the paper covering it had been brought to him in. The oldest books among his collection had begun to rot and while he was trapped within the walls of this place, he intended on rewriting them as he went along, if nothing more than for Marris's benefit. Of course, this time he'd a few more tricks up his sleeve, blessing the paper and bindings of this newest book, before he wrote a single word within its pages. All it took was having it in his hands and a small amount of concentration, after all. Even though the parchment of all his oldest writings literally fell apart within the hands of whoever held it, not a word on any of the pages legible any longer, he knew each sentence of each book by heart. If course, he'd lived it, every memory as vivid as the day it happened. The oldest among his writings having been written after the invention of paper, many years before that the information simply sitting in his head waiting for the day when he might have the ability to record it. Once something new was created beyond paper, he supposed he'd have to rewrite it all over again. Until then, the spell would protect the integrity of the paper from now forward. After all, what was a few thousand years in the grand scheme of things? He could have just blessed the texts onto the pages of each new book, however something in placing the handwritten script on each of the pages himself had always been more gratifying and soothing. Pulling a special quill from his jacket pocket, he opened the freshly made, leather bound, book beginning to place word to page. His mind filing through old memories while he did so, thinking about those first days, as he did every time he wrote down his written history and the spells that he'd learned in his many, many years. One would be amazed at what memories the mind could truly hold, if trained to do so, it was still quite the marvel, even after all this time.

"In the beginning, when the gods began to create the realms, they were experimental. In choosing the races of this world, they deemed some successful and some unsuccessful. The most dangerous of them, they destroyed. Those they felt harmless, though some flawed, they allowed to live. The Humani were created closer to the end of creation, just before the creation of humans themselves. We were more perfect than humans, all of their greatest qualities with few of their weaknesses. However, the gods soon learned that perfection, in itself, was among the greatest flaws of all. Not only did my kind become blasphemous, reveling in our supremacy, but much like humans we became abundant, multiplying and consuming everything in our wake. Until, not only was a younger race created, similar with a few more imperfections of our own, but after which a secondary race was also created, to hunt us into extinction...the vampires. One must have a turnable race to create the cursed species, after all, and the gods created them to have a particular fondness for the blood of the Humani. I, myself, was able to dodge the young race of hunters long enough to where I have become stronger than most of the younger vampires, as I've thousands of years on majority. However, still there are a few that could bring our race to extinction. Most of those that are left of that original creation, have no desire to hunt us any longer, having lived long enough by now that they either do not care or I have found ways to restrain them from doing so. However, unfortunately, there is still at least one of them that I know of out there that still hunts us to this day, one of the few creatures that still remembers how to do away with my race entirely. As most of the Humani have been hunted down and terminated, as far as I'm aware, there are no more left beyond myself. Though I have been in hiding for a very long time now and if there were any left, I'm sure they would be doing much the same, while I have been at the Albatross, a place protected from the undead by strong spells, I have listened across the realms for their voices. I have not heard a single living thought among those I knew still to exist. Whether they have lost all hope and are no longer listening or they have all gone to the life beyond, I do not know, however I am inclined to believe that I might have at least heard something within these last few days, if in fact any of my people were left out there. This is disheartening, after all a creature without a race is truly the loneliest soul in all of the realms.'

Sorin closed the book, after he had written these things, having added to his original writings, as he always tended to do, revisions were always the greatest evolution of one's memoirs. It was time for him to open the doors for the day to the lounge and dining room. He had been notified of the position within the guarded Inn, by way of traveling messenger, having been on the lookout for such a position where the man could once again live something of a normal lifestyle, able to once again be out in the open and enjoy the luxury that came along with having a purpose. Having found the little misguided witch on his way here, had been an unexpected side note that he would likely include in more current journals. She, much like himself, a refugee without a people to call her own or lend her protection, so he had taken her under his tutelage. Sorin having decided to guide her to the ability to eventually take care of herself and the ability to set out on her own one day. She was quite the beauty and Sorin had been taken with her, from the moment he'd set eyes upon her, his fondness only growing the longer he knew her. However, he left that fondness where it lie, considering her a mere child in his eyes and where she would eventually grow old and die, as was the destiny of every member of her race, he would not. Through his many millennia he had seen hundreds of girls, just like this one, his soft heart having fallen for them and watched as they quickly became frail and died, making his heart mostly hard and cold to all things mortal. So it was that since, he watched from afar, caring for the girl and teaching her, but nothing more.

Management of the Albatross Inn was easy for the man, considering he'd done the same countless times, evolving his practices as he went to suit the times. He had given Marris the job of waitress and housekeeping, teaching the girl discipline, along with the magic lessons he gave her in the evenings. The two lived in the same suite, as she often studied his journals by candlelight late into the night, which he didn't mind, in fact, it almost made him proud that she found such fondness in reading them and if something were to ever happen to him, likely he would pass them on to her, hopefully with a completeness that wasn't quite there at the moment.

As he opened the doors of the dining hall, he began to shake his head, glancing around at the leftovers from the past evening. 'Sterling.' The young man had much to learn and was much more careless than Sorin truly liked, however the boy would generate new patrons and business. Sorin, though he might come to regret the decision, had hired the boy because he saw a bit of himself in him somehow. Lost and alone, running from something the young one wouldn't exactly say, mostly brawn, but seeming as if he had had to be in his short life. With superhuman speed, Sorin gathered up what had been left out and straightened up the dining room and bar that was still slightly in the process of redecoration. In fact, the whole Inn was in the process of redecoration now that Sorin had taken control of management. Master of evolution of being, Sorin had noticed the outdated wall-papers and unsanded floors, hiring an entire crew of carpenters to refresh and repair the aging Inn. He'd gotten Feather's blessing by messenger, how they always communicated, and though he was paying for the revisions out of his own well lined pocket, he expected great returns on his investment. It wasn't that Sorin needed the money, considering his race excelled in business affairs and all number of other things, Sorin needed the normalcy of an every day life. He craved day to day tasks and purpose, after all, what was an eternity of life worth without actually living it?

The Trouble with Young Witches Learning Old Spells

(LARGE SCALE GAME: BEGINNING POST [UNPLAYED] – 2016 – GETTING RID OF OLD GHOSTS)

Marris had lit the candles one by one, not quite strong enough with the elements to light them all at once like Sorin often did for her. He was making nightly rounds and at the moment, she purposely began this ritual by herself. Earlier that day, before her shift in the dining room, she had been reading through one of the older of Sorin's books, finding a spell that caught her interest. Sorin would have never allowed her to do the spell, if he'd been there with her, claiming that she wasn't strong enough to cast such spells as were written in the books because he had not taught her enough basics quiet yet. However, Marris, being young and strong minded, didn't see what one little spell would hurt. This particular spell was something she'd thought about for some time, waiting until she could find herself alone for a period of time.

Once she had everything ready for the ritual, she sat down cross-legged on the floor in front of the book. She picked the athame up from beside her, making a deep cut along the palm of her opposite hand, blood welling up behind the cut quickly. She slowly placed her hands palm to palm, in an almost praying fashion, beginning to speak the incantation that was written on the pages of Sorin's journal, sliding her palms up and down to allow the blood to cover the entirety of her palms and fingers. Marris repeated the incantation over and over as she brought both hands to her temples, creating a bloody fingerprint with her index fingers. Next, she moved her hands, crossing them in front of her as she made a second set of bloody fingerprints index fingers, each on the opposite shoulder of the hand that had touched them. For the third set of fingerprints, she uncrossed her arms and merely placed both hands flat on her knees, causing bloody hand prints underneath where they lie. It wasn't long after her hands touched her knees that the flames of the candles flared once, then went out.

"Hello?" Marris whispered into the darkness, with no answer. However, with a sudden gasp escaping her, a blinding light pierced through the center of her body, opening a portal that covered the majority of her torso. The light began to pulse, throwing her head back, eyes glassing over for a moment, as the flashes shook her body with every time they generated. Sorin felt the imbalance of energy within the hotel almost instantly and with every bit of inhuman speed he had in him, raced to their shared room, forcing open the locked door with a blast of magical energy. As his eyes fell upon the scene of the girl with the portal open through the center of her body, a momentary cringe came over his face, before throwing himself down by her side.

'Stupid girl.' He thought to himself. In truth though, he slightly blamed himself, allowing her to go through the books at will and not keeping her under constant watched while she was looking through them. Sorin brought his hands up, seeming to begin to contain the beating light, forcing the portal closed slowly, putting as much strength as he possibly could into it, so as to close the portal as soon as he possibly could. When finally the light went out, Marris's body fell to the floor with a loud thud, and Sorin gathered her up into his arms, still sitting on the floor and leaning back onto a piece of furniture.

'This is going to be a fun adventure.' He thought to himself, considering the portal to the other side she had opened had remained so long enough to let several tormented souls through, throwing off the balance of energy within the inn. Because of the powerful wards, the spirits she had let free would not be able to exit the building, however he was going to need help. He would make all the necessary arrangements to contain each spirit as they were found, while he created and maintained a one way portal back to where they had come from. He hoped he could entrust Sterling to lead this search throughout the building, because Marris would be out of commission for a few days after the amount of energy the experience had taken from her. Sorin stood, picking the girl up as he did, taking her to her bed. He laid her down, covering her with her blankets, and pulling her hair away from her face. It was a good thing he cared for the girl, because that sort of recklessness could end up harming himself, his staff, and their patrons. By the time she awoke, he'd likely have her mess cleaned up, but he could only hope that this would be a learning experience for her.

Sorin moved to his own room, beginning to form the golden boxes that would contain the spirits as they were found. He blessed each to entrap a spirit with a single word from those that might participate in the hunt. He would have to send a messenger to announce it in the morning paper, as this was a task of a timely manner. If they weren't able to get the spirits contained and soon, they might eventually find their way outside of the inn or worse, hurt someone in or outside of the protection wards. Sorin couldn't allow this incident to effect his business and he hoped that there would be quite the turnout for the hunt. He wouldn't advertise it as a problem, but a venture of entertainment purposes, ghost hunting for sport. Exactly, that was the answer to this situation. Sorin continued into the night creating plenty of the blessed golden boxes, considering he was unsure of just how many spirits had escaped, but he was ready for the hoard as soon as the sun rose the next morning.

Barrier Falls: House of Cards

(COMIC BOOK START (WITHOUT IMAGES) - 2011 - WRITTEN FOR KEVIN)

Morning breaks. Just another Monday, dreams fall through the cracks of life, dreams of what could be…what would have been.

Every day the inside flows out, through tears of memories, once lived, lost through bloodshed and broken lives. Senseless the need for an end, but I never knew how I would need you if you weren't there.

Darkness fails to comfort, but brings back shadows of the past. Lives that can't be returned and lies that can't be rectified. Happy once wasn't so far away, but close enough not to be seen. Wasted time trying to defer madness through friendship.

How could I stop? These reasons too simple to understand, but complex enough to be heard by unlistening ears. Lie to me again, because I miss the sound. It's been so long since I heard the voice of reason.

Those cold arms aren't there to wrap around, will they be again? Bloody, cold, lying arms…

…with boundaries crossed, broken promises kept, but unknown. How could you take the moon with you knowing I would feel its absence so strong?

In broken hearts honesty found, colors fade to grey, as

another day passes without that shining light. Burning bright the fires, the hands of Hell grasp, choking me in their tight hold…

"Broken lies, lives, burn bright…unending…"

Shadows dance around as if joyous of the lingering hours, that seem to tick on for an eternal day. Moments turn to years, but time holds firm as the clock merely chimes away another midnight.

How can I bear another sunrise? Another day of realization, another afternoon of loneliness and sorrow. The memories of life and loss that tear at me like knives, slicing pieces from my shattered soul.

A single set of footprints follow me where once were yours. Beside me, step for step in tune with the silent heartbeat of the living world…until there were no more.

What if I couldn't take another step? What would happen if my broken heart ceased to beat? If I took no other breath and slipped into eternal slumber? Would you be there in my dreams? Waiting… Are you waiting for me just beyond that border between life and death?

And if it happened that you could not be there to greet me in that world beyond this one, would it all be for not? No. Even if I could never set my eyes on your beautiful face, if I never felt your hand heavy against my own I could not bear this world without… Never ending darkness consume my soul, take away the pain of life, chase away these tears, and fill my emptiness with dreamless sleep.

Vison fades and memories blur as the pain begins to dull.

Restricted movement, darkness creeping in the world around me begins to slip away.

Final dying breaths, labored by a heavy chest, a cast shadow begs my eyes to focus. A trace of a ghost, a being that didn't belong. Life between two worlds. A soul apart. Rebellious silhouette against a blinding light.

Familiar voice shattering the silence and lips of ice press forward, soft and damp, like dew drops on satin in early spring. This kiss... This kiss. Full of life and love, bringing me choking back to old comforts and new vision.

"Kept Comforts, realization of light once lost...forever treasured for a life well saved."

Forced Happiness

(POETRY – 2006 – PUBLISHED UNDER THE PEN NAME FOXF1R3_V1XON)

What if I left tomorrow?
Walked down the street and kept walking
Would you care? Notice that I'm not there?
I'm screaming inside. Can you hear it?
Are you listening? Don't you miss me?
Don't you see me? I'm standing in front of you
You're looking through me
Sadness, confusion
Wrapped in illusion
Of the forced smiles
Of a happy life, full of strife
Endless arguments
Cunt, bitch, push, shove
You've put out our light, extinguished my fire
Bruised and broken
Mind, body, and soul
I can't believe I couldn't see
What your love has done to me
Where am I? Am I dreaming?
Is this my nightmare?
My life, my hell, my frequent blank stare
Echoes of what he says, what you say
Maybe someday, you might treat me that way
Can I wait? Should I stay?

Is it worth the high price that I pay?
This nothingness, emptiness, self-doubt
Disgust, distrust, this shell that I've become
And then again, maybe it's not him
But is it you? Feeling this way for the rest of my life?
What do I do? Everything's unclear
This worth I feel, beautiful, after six years renewed
I don't want to say the words, I know you don't want
to hear
Sadness, confusion
Wrapped in the illusion
The forced smiles
Of a happy life…

Summer Sun

(POETRY – 2007 - PUBLISHED UNDER THE PEN NAME FOXF1R3_V1XON)

Seasons change and seasons pass
Forcing me to forget the past
Forgetting all my reasons
My reasons for my change of seasons
Summer burns the lonely days
Long and weary in many ways
Dreaming of the Winter gone
The snow and ice has held so long
Where has the Spring gone?
The Fall days, the rising sun
Something missing
Something wrong
Something in me
Left with the set of the Summer sun.

My World

(POETRY - 2009)

Paint me in a shade of grey
So I might reach yet another day
Abstract in your mind's display
Twisted in the words you say
Mindless mockery
of a tasteless dream
Shadow of a world
That is more than what it seems
Reach inside and find
It's all within my mixed up mind
Unknown, Go home
You're not alone
Take me down, without a sound
Pound me to the ground
Just for bein' 'round
Change of heart, before you even start
Nice to know, before you go
Allow me to show, another side of me.
Risin' from the ashes of a broken life
Scattered, littered, plagued with endless strife
Phoenix breaking from the flames
I always change inside, but forever look the same.

Every Time

(POETRY – APPROX. 2010)

Every time I make up my mind,
Something Changes.
Every time I do something good,
Nobody sees.
Every time I feel like I care,
Nobody's there.
Every time I think I'm in control,
I fall apart.
Every time I try to rise above,
I fall back down.
Every time my skies are blue,
It starts to rain.
Every time I look at him,
I cry.
Because every time he looks at me,
He smiles.

My Paper Heart

(POETRY - 2010)

Scattered memories of the words that never were,
Could fill a book of things I could have said before,
Honestly, promise me, that this will never die,
To bleed again and see my heart may tell me lies,
Your subtle visions never cast aside but falling on empty eyes,
I want to see if you're tell me, but on sight I can't rely,
Just let me know if when I go I still linger on your mind,
If the way things are might not stay the same, I'll let these secrets lie,
Throw my words to the wind, watching as they fall and I die again today,
Because it's killing me to let it be these things I want to say,
You bring me to that place inside where the world just fades away,
I watch you go, but you don't know how bad I want to stay,
Moving slow, expectations low, Just take away the dark,
Fade away the pain, tell me it's not in vain, will you hold my paper heart?
I'm running out of excuses why you are running through my mind,
Trying to find a reason to spend a bit more time,
Kind of like a fever my addiction to you
Fueling these flames with every single move,
Stars fall from the sky with thoughts of you,
Tempting, ever so gently to make my wish come true,

Honestly, promise me that this will never die,
Don't let this die...
This feeling I hold in side...
Don't let it...
I won't let it die.

Rapid Cycle

(POETRY - 2011)

Broken bottles,
Broken dreams,
Litter layers of asphalt scenes.
Time begins,
And time also ends,
Rapid cycle, twists and bends.
Trash and treasure,
Nature's pleasure,
Overgrown beyond measure.
Pad your feet,
Plant your seat,
Listen to the silent beat.
Dumpster drums pound,
Yarn guitars play their sound,
To listening ears for miles around.
Sing that pitiful song,
One to which we sing along,
Play that melody all day long.
Revolving like doors,
Walking dirt floors,
Screaming, shouting, wanting more.
Rusty stage,
Turn another page,
As another band begins to play.

Caged Bird

(POETRY - 2016)

The emotion flows out
Through ribbons of self doubt
Caged bird
Unable to be heard
The song of my soul
It's tune so sorrowful
And yet...
Yet I keep going
Keep moving
Keep seeing
Keep believing
Hoping to find something brilliant in a world so dull
Heart after heart I touch shattering with the depth of my pull
Cursed to leave monsters in my wake
Forced to feel the pain of every demon I create
I've constructed a wall around my heart
But brick by brick I'm always tearing it apart
Time after time
I commit my crime
Building stronger walls, more ice
I push away, trying to play nice
Concealing my depths to appear hollow inside
Until such a day I might find no reason to hide
Only Fate knows what will be

As for today, it's not for me to see
No matter, come what may
Behind those walls, still beats, even to this day.

Seven Deadly

(NOVEL START [UNFINISHED] - 2014)

Chapter 1

Night falls over New Salem City like a plague. It seeps into every crevice, its darkness consuming everything in its path. New Salem, where the old world and the new world collide. A world where lifelong secrets could be in the open because of the city's position beneath the geographic world.

Seven Deadly glanced around at the city beneath him, then up toward the man-made sky. Clear. Stars, the same as last night and the night before and a million nights before that. The monotony was enough to make a person sick, and the sadness of what remained was that nothing was more imperfect or corrupt than a society built on perfection.

With a single leap, he fell several stories to the ground, reaching out in front of him to a spread crouch. Standing, his eyeless sockets moved over the area, searching for the pulsing red tones of evil in the underground valley. The magical façade kept his identity hidden, skeletal and intimidating to the naked eye. In truth, it was only a mask. The man beneath it vulnerable and mortal.

He stood there, in the shadow of the streetlight, until a familiar glow caught his attention. Red mist, bright as sunlight and thick as molasses, the aura of evil unmistakable. Moving in closer, he watched.

Only a novice would run in without accessing the situation and when the sinner revealed themselves, he relaxed. The woman couldn't have been younger than eighty, her long grey hair falling down around her shoulders like a sparkling white river. To the untrained eye, she would seem a normal retiree living out her days in the quiet solitary of old age. To Seven Deadly, she was the villain. Though at the age she was now, she could not defend herself any longer, nor could she do any more damage to the world, but her soul was forever marked. It was these markings he saw, the scars of sin, the embellishments of good deeds, and the numb fragments of complacency. Only careful examination would show just what this woman had done that had marked her so harshly, but her soul was tarnished, endlessly tainted and with the transition of death quickly upon her, her red soul would be in turmoil for the rest of eternity.

It didn't do any good to slaughter them all, this woman likely had a few years left to breathe through her guilt, and the punishment for her crimes would be far worse than any torture he could ever inflict upon her. Call it hell, call it heaven, call it what you like, the mind takes you where you need to be. When the physical body is dead and the soul is all that's left, the soul creates its own existence, great or terrible depending on the mindset of the deceased.

His focus moved on. There were many, many more threats beyond that of an old woman tonight. He could feel the auras as they pulsed around him, scattering the city like a colony of ants, imprints of their damaged souls burning bullet holes in his mind. After mere moments of passing through darkened alley ways and the shadows of looming brick buildings, another aura caught his eye. Green. The green ones were tough to decipher, the decision of action not always a choice between black and white, many shades of grey accompanied a green aura.

The green aura of sickness was almost always benign. Sickness of mind, sickness of body, sickness of heart, but there were times when sickness had need of being judged. There were times when sickness walked hand in hand with wrath, lust, greed... Just because the aura hadn't turned red, didn't mean it wasn't about to. Through the cover of the night itself, Seven Deadly watched, those deep abysmal pits focusing on the girl beneath the street light. He knew what she was, it was obvious. The short thin dress barely covered her and left nothing to mystery. In another life, he might have looked on her much differently, but in the one he now lived, he knew she was waiting to pass on death.

The vigilante had previously been compared to Jack the Ripper, which of course, he found humorous. The difference between the two was obvious; Jack the Ripper had no agenda, no purpose for his shameless torturing. The diseases these whores carried killed millions. Passed on and passed on from the sinners that lusted for them to the innocent who loved the sinners. He had seen the cycle before. Deadly viruses passed in the name of love, defiling what the term stood for, until nothing remained in the heart of the innocent but anger and mistrust. Green could turn a blue neutral to a red threat in mere seconds.

This girl was young, late teens by the look of it, but disease written all over her. She was thin, so thin that her bones protruded from her body like fossils on a creek bed. Her skin pulled tight against them, lacking the luster of a healthy individual. Just what sickness she carried was unclear. Seven

Deadly was not a telepath, nor did he have divine assistance, he could merely discern a good soul from an evil soul.

His movement toward her was quick, yet silent, a predator hunting unsuspecting prey. His movements were fluid, much more so than one would expect a skeletal figure to move. However, because it was a mere illusion, his muscles toned and experienced underneath the fabric cloak and magical shield.

Suddenly, he was upon her, gaunt fingers wrapping around her neck and pressing her against the wooden pole of the streetlight. The girl hung staring into the empty eyes of his skull, wriggling slightly, fear coursing through her, making her green aura pulse.

Seven Deadly held her, careful to let her breathe, but holding firm so she could not get away. The touch of his hand against her, his black aura blending with hers, allowed him to read her soul like Cliff's Notes. She knew she had the virus, she had given it to others night after night, men and women, whoever paid for her next fix. She was sick and dying, not only from addiction to the drugs, but the disease she carried inside of her. It was a matter of time before someone found her in a gutter...but instead her time was now. Her aura wasn't red, because those she had infected had not passed, possibly they didn't even know and until their untimely deaths, her aura would merely remain of green.

It was these injustices that he fought against, the injustices of morality, the crimes that the law did not protect against. Hookers kept no records of their charges; there was no way for these johns to check their hired booty call for disease; there was no way of protecting wives, girlfriends, husbands, and boyfriends from the horrors that these whores produced. The girl squirmed and whined, but her cries fell on deaf ears. It was the glint of reflected light on polished metal that caused her to begin screaming, she knew her end was near. He shoved her hard against the light pole, knocking the breath out of her and causing her to quiet.

When he spoke to her, his voice was deep and emotionless. "You have been judged..." With those few words, the blade in his opposite hand slid swiftly over her neck, cutting so deep that her head immediately fell backward, the gash gaping open, blood pouring to the ground around them.

Seven Deadly dropped the lifeless body of the diseased girl to the ground, letting it fall in a bloody pile. The green glow of her aura had already begun to fade as the gurgle of air from her lungs bubbled through bloody vocal cords. She would be a threat no longer. Wen the luminescence of her soul had completely vanished, he pulled a card from the rags of the cloak that he wore. The card was empty and white, however when he tossed it down on her body and the thick paper soaked up the bright red blood, a single word appeared bring white against the pool of red. 'Lust.'

The woman was already dead inside, it didn't matter much that he relieved her soul from its earthly prison. Day after day he searched through blue neutral to blue neutral, a handful of purple auras dotted his vision, but it wasn't them that bothered him. His thoughts couldn't help but wonder how long before the neutrals that he passed would become something more. Every day colors in the spectrum shifted, like a time card, a person would punch out of neutral. Sometimes it only took a single event to go from blue to red, other times multiple events and color shifts.

Red was always Seven Deadly's main concern, it meant that the person within the aura had to be removed immediately. It meant they had already committed some of the worst sins possible and, if not stopped, were likely to continue. The spectrum was fairly broad and a rainbow of colors, but within the few months that he had begun seeing the colors, it had been easy to figure out.

A blue aura was a neutral, a person that was basically good, lived a good life and surrounded themselves with good people. Purple meant that a person was in constant exposure to sin, but continued to remain in more of a neutral spectrum. These two categories were what the average citizen fell into. Green auras, like the woman he had met this evening, were deadly sicknesses. Whether they be sickness of body, such as cancers or other terminal illnesses; or mental illnesses, causing suicidal or homicidal thoughts. Many times the person was not at fault for a green aura, after all, how could you really blame someone for having cancer. However alcoholism, prostitution, obesity, drug abuse these things Seven Deadly considered closer to choices than to sicknesses.

Yellow was always a red flag, as was orange. Yellow meant that a person had entered a lifestyle of complete selfishness, uncaring of those around them, even the people that cared about them the most. This was always the first step to red. At times, yellows could change. Yellows could become a blue neutral again, but the closer they became to red the less likely it was for them to go backward again. Orange always meant that the person had made the decision to commit a deadly sin. Their mind had moved on from just selfish fantasy toward a plan of action and it was just a matter of time, before orange became red. Once red, there was no going back. Repentance was futile. No amount of apologies could bring the murdered back from the dead or undo the damage of a rape. Red was intentional, red was premeditated, cold and emotionless. Red was a death sentence, a person living on stolen time. The colors were a spectrum to go by, the human life force; the insignia of the human soul.

However, there were exceptions. Three exceptions, to be exact. White, black, and grey. Seven Deadly's own soul was black. He was a peacekeeper. A soul designated to be nulled. His soul was all colors, yet it was none, because he committed sin to prevent sin. He was designated a killer for the greater good. He hadn't been born with it, but hadn't truly chosen it either. It had chosen him. The world had chosen him to be her protector. It was as if a jury of the dead, souls pooled after death, had chosen him to make sure that the world would go on, continue along a decent path. He wasn't the only black soul in the world, but there were few. Quitting wasn't an option. Quitting meant that he would be flagged. Black status stripped from him would mean the brightest red possible and his eternity in torment. Black status stripped was the worst of all fates.

White auras would be what the religious would consider angels; those with a pure soul. Babies are born with white auras, their future yet to be decided, their souls not yet tarnished by the way of the world. Few are those who never tarnish, who go through life with a pure white soul. Saints, prophets, messiahs, these are those with a white soul. They go through life showing others the way back to blue, setting an example and coaxing others to follow a better path. It has been said that if a pure white soul found a red soul truly worthy of their help, they could even turn a red to blue. Possible, but not likely in Seven Deadly's experience.

Grey souls were tricky. Grey souls watched. They weren't truly on any spectrum, because they were not truly, bad nor good. They were those who could see whether a person could be saved or must be destroyed. Grey souls were the embodiment of patience. Emotionless, but hopeful. Grey was also special for one major reason, they too had a spectrum; and though they hardly ever moved on that scale, a grey could become any shade they liked at any time; from helpful and hopeful to dangerous and deadly within moments if necessary.

It had always been said that white and black souls could become a grey soul, but the likeliness was slim. In other words, it had never happened. White souls were white because that was the way they were made, hopeful and caring, created to care for the world and make it a better place. Black souls were the enforcers, created to keep the peace through disposal of those who would create chaos and destruction. White souls were pure because not even their thoughts could color their aura in any way. Black souls were dark, because their thoughts were prone to violence and doubt.

Seven Deadly had seen life. He had seen what the world did to people and what people did to it. There was no hope. Blue turned to yellow, yellow to orange, and orange to red. The cycle was endless, uncontrollable, and inevitable. There was no stopping it or slowing it. Every blue neutral he saw would either die or turn, that was the way of life; that was human nature. The nature of a human life was sin.

Chapter 2

Robert Ketterick Bishop. The man of the hour. A man's man, a ladies man, as famous in his personal life as he was in his police profile. A punk rich kid, grown to a frivolous carefree lifestyle.

The history of the Bishops in New Salem City, was the history of New Salem itself. Born from the Herricks, founders of the sub-level city, his namesake the son of Amos Herrick, was the founder of New Salem. The city of Salem, Massachusetts had always been known for its history of witch trials. Tourism flourished based on the humorous idea that genocide was committed on account of the paranoid delusions of religious zealots. In truth, any intelligent person should have been able to see that someone born to such power would never allow themselves to be burnt at the stake. It was a completely ridiculous concept, but it served the Herrick family well. Hidden amongst society, the powerful line of witches flourished, until science surpassed the common knowledge. Science was the true enemy of magic, religion was a mere annoyance. It was science that forced the Herricks and many like them underground, quite literally.

New Salem City was founded on the basis of sanctuary, asylum for the scientifically unexplainable. New Salem was protection for those who wanted a normal life, but were abnormal from society. The Herricks, needing refuge from a constantly changing world, where long life and strange powers would make them stand out in a world now full of cameras and records. Most within the city had dual citizenship, able to live in Old Salem above ground, but release themselves from the bindings of secrecy below ground if they chose to. For some, the underground was a permanent existence. Some were mandated to live below ground, because a life in the geographical world was impossible. Some hadn't the monetary sources to support a dual existence. Most on the surface hadn't any idea of the city beneath their feet, but those below knew all too well what the surface life held.

RK Bishop was one of the chosen few allowed to live a double life, above and below the surface. Most from both worlds knew of him, his fame as the only son of Hartford Bishop preceded him everywhere he went. Like the Paris Hilton of the magical realm, he had bullshitted his way through life, without a thought or care. It was also this lifestyle and the choices he had made in his twenty six years that delivered him into a world that was unexpected, even in a world full of wonders.

RK slammed his hand down on the blaring alarm clock, peering through the haze of a hangover at the red digital numbers ahead of him. The noise that it produced had stopped, but the looming fact that he would have to begin his day kept his mind from settling into sleep once again. He buried his face in his pillow, laying there for several minutes, before the alarm once again began its shrill whine. This time the clock was swatted to the floor, where it continued to squeal. Rob sat up on the edge of his bed, scratching through his hair, forcing it to lightly tap against his shoulders.

Instead of once again turning the alarm off, he merely left it, moving into his attached en suite to do his morning business. When he was finished, he didn't even bother picking up his phone from the nightstand or getting dressed, he merely grabbed a red, silk robe from the closet and made his way downstairs.

The house itself was in the messy disarray of a typical bachelor pad, not filthy by any means, but certainly not in order. RK made his way to the kitchen, picking a few different mugs off of the counter and glancing inside of them, before deciding one was clean enough to put day old coffee in. It was cold, of course, but the taste and caffeine were still there. It didn't matter; he wasn't awake enough yet for it to matter. He moved through to his living room, slowly sitting down on the couch so as not to spill his breakfast. He set the cup down on the end table next to him and began digging through the couch cushions for the remote, it was almost always hidden somewhere random. He quickly found it, turned the TV on, and began flipping casually through the channels.

This was his normal morning routine, truthfully, not morning, as it was already almost noon. His phone would be blowing up soon, as those within the bar crowd were likely waking up just the same as he. With his cell upstairs, he could be free to enjoy some quiet contemplation of the night before, at least what he could remember of it. He sat there in merely boxers, socks, and a robe until he had smoked a couple of cigarettes and the magic of the caffeinated beverage worked its way through his veins. An event that was almost unfortunate, because it meant it was time to begin the day.

RK tossed the remote on the couch as he made his way back

up the stairs. He heard his phone vocalizing its demands when he was merely halfway up, beeping and ringing with ferocity. He ignored it. He wasn't going to be bothered with that mess just yet; he'd listen to voicemails and read text messages after his shower.

It didn't take long to shower, it never really did, and when he was finished he grabbed a t-shirt from the closet and picked up a pair of jeans from the floor. He brought them up to his nose, making sure the smell of a few days of wear didn't linger on them. He shrugged, tossing them on. It was then that he picked up the flashing phone, pressing the button to listen.

"You have…twelve new messages. Message one. 'Hey babe, its Carry. I know it's a bit early, but I was wanting to know if you wanted to meet my…'" He didn't allow the message to play through before pressing the delete button firmly.

"Message two. 'Sup, my man, just got a new shine in the show room, got Bishop tattooed all over it, man…sub system so tight it'll blow the pannies off of any bitch walks in front 'o it, man. Holla at yo boy.'" King sold motor vehicles and though RK had only ever bought machines with two wheels from him, it seemed he was always trying to get him to buy some sort of four wheeled monster. It didn't make much sense to RK, but the guy was persistent.

"Message three. ' Hiya! Uh…you don't know me, but this is Tiffany, you wrote your number in sharpie on me last night…um…' The voice giggled for a moment before she continued. 'You wrote it on my boob.' Some more girl giggling. 'Just wondered if you wanted to go for din—'" Delete. Nope, RK knew where this kind of message lead and it wasn't somewhere he wanted to ride with that one.

The rest of the messages were very similar and he listened to them as he was combing through his hair. Nothing important, nothing urgent, truthfully nothing that really mattered that much.

Rob closed the door behind him, turning the handle to make sure it was locked. He made his way down the sidewalk, tossing his keys in his hand as he walked. The sliding garage door was already open, he had made sure when he had still been inside. The beautiful red 929 glittered with the sunlight that seeped through the garage door.

"Good morning, baby girl..." RK cooed to the bike, the only lady in his life that remained a constant. She truly was a stunning machine. 954cc engine capacity, 68lbs of torque, zero to sixty in 3.3 seconds, she really was the love of his life. He'd pushed her to almost two hundred miles per hour, though she was only listed at one seventy eight on performance specs. He slid into the seat of the bike, caressing the tank with his fingertips. She purred like a kitten when he started her up, as if responding to his touch.

Living Beyond the Midwest

(AUTOBIOGRAPHY START [ROUGH AND UNFINISHED] - 2016)

It's difficult to remember a good majority of my childhood. I have bits and pieces, as we all do. I do remember the hill I used to hide behind when I was very young. I hid there so that I wouldn't have to come inside when it began to get dark, thinking my mother couldn't see me behind it. My father had planted fruit trees on that hill, though he'd had difficulty getting them to survive. My parents were still young then too. This wasn't our first home, however I can't remember the house we lived in when I was first born. I was born in Kirksville, Missouri at Grim Smith Hospital at 11:11 in the morning. I was my parents first child, born to them after a few years of marriage, the true product of my parents' love for each other. My father, for as long as I can remember worked for the BNSF railroad and my mother worked for a small chiropractic clinic in the town of Kahoka. The first home we lived in was several miles outside of town, my parents rented it from my great-grandparents, as it was the home that my mother's mother had grown up in.

My great-grandparents had owned the home. They had managed to raise seven children in that tiny farmhouse. The story of my great-grandmother is a sad one, one full of heartache, but ending in the joy of a large and beautiful family. My great-grandmother was born Gladys Mae Wilson August 1st, 1905. ________ At the very young age of 1X she was rejected by her family and with only a trunk full of possessions, was sent out into the world, destitute and alone. She ______ until she was xx years old, it was then that she met her first love Frank Harmon. He was the love of her life, however their fairytale love was short-lived. In 19XX, both Gladys and Frank contracted smallpox. Both husband and wife fought the disease together, however by the time my great-grandmother awoke, her beloved had already passed on. Again, she was alone in the world, until she found my Great-Grandfather Wells 'Frank' Sanders. He was XX her senior and had been married before, his wife had passed away ________ leaving him and his two young daughters without a woman in their life. Though she still held the love for her first husband tight in her heart, she allowed herself to love again marrying him and accepting his two daughters, Garnet and Mary, as her own.

I remember Toby and Wendy, the children of our nearest neighbors that were just up the hill. I couldn't have been much older than two or three years of age. I used to play with them, as they lived just down the road. I remember the 'tree house' that they had, that wasn't really in a tree, but it was still fun to pretend. I remember the pantry I slept in the house we lived in then. The pantry that my parents had made into a bedroom off of the kitchen, because I didn't want to sleep in my actual bedroom upstairs. There were wasps in there. Even after my parents assured me that they were gone, to me, as little as I was, the upstairs room was still scary. At that time we lived in a little 'town' called Chambersburg, which wasn't really a town, more like a grouping of rural houses out in the middle of nowhere. We lived about fifteen minutes from the nearest store or business in general. I remember the barn cats that used to roam around, most of them wild, but when there was a litter of tame ones I had always claimed them for my own, wanting to keep every last one, even though I knew we couldn't. I remember lying in a plastic children's pool, with a blanket in it, in a sweater and rain boots, holding onto the very last kitten we had left from one year's litter, pleading with my mother to just keep this one. We couldn't though and I knew that, but I was very young, so at that time I didn't really understand why.

I remember climbing the trees outside of our house and outside of my grandparents house, on both sides. There were so many things I remember getting into that I don't believe my parents ever even knew about. I'm not sure if I was as mischievous as my own children are now, but I was fairly close.

(Restart)

When I was born we lived outside of a small town in Missouri, in a house owned by my great-grandparents, that my parents rented monthly. My dad worked for the BNSF railroad and my mother for a small chiropractic clinic with a big reputation. The doctor in that clinic could work miracles, at least, from what we could see, anything that ailed you he had a treatment or a fix for...and it worked, sometimes within hours, sometimes within days, but it always worked. There are days now that I wish times were still like they were back then, just so that I would possibly have a fix for the way things are. However, times always do and have changed.

I was a fairly normal kid growing up. I fed mud mixed with

cat food to the cats, pretending I was cooking and feeding dinner to my 'children'. Sometimes the cats tolerated me, sometimes they didn't, but back then those barn cats ate a lot of mud. If you would ask the man of the house now, he would tell you that my cooking hasn't gotten much better since, even though I'm a great cook, he's just a picky eater.

My baby sister was born when I was five and a half years old. I barely remember pieces of the day my parents brought her home. I had been staying at my grandmother's house, my father's mother, because my mother's parents had wanted to be there with her at the hospital. I remember how small she looked, just like a doll, and how special I felt that I was a big sister now. Though, eventually she got bigger and I didn't feel as proud, when I found my dolls without heads, hidden behind the living room furniture. My sister and I never did have much in common and though here and there we've had a somewhat rocky foundation to our relationship, strained because of a five year age gap, we've always been able to settle things out eventually.

I remember the many times that my sister did things that I thought were just the craziest things ever, like when she had just started crawling, she somehow backed her way off of the porch of our new house, to where her head caught in the railing and she got stuck there. Back then, you didn't really think about baby proofing things or making things certain lengths so things like that didn't happen. I'm fairly positive that those type of safety devices were created because of children like my sister. She once piled all of the toys that she owned in her closet, just to reach something on the very top shelf. Who knows what it might have been, because she ended up on the floor, with all of her toys piled on top of her. On her first day of school, my mother made sure to give them every bit of emergency information she had because she knew something was going to happen. Sure enough, on the first day of kindergarten, my sister ran into the wall of the gym and knocked herself out cold. She was alright, but certainly very bold and brave from the very beginning.

In contrast to my sister, I was fairly timid when I began school. The first time my mother tried to put me in kindergarten, it wasn't quite the right fit. They told my mother that I was right on the cusp of the age cut off and they believed I was too young and not physically ready to begin school. Even though, by the age of five I was already reading and writing, something many of the other kids were still barely learning. That was also back when kindergarteners only went half days anyway, so when the teacher or whoever it was said that I was not quite be ready for a half day of school it was apparently significant enough to my parents that they pulled me out of school after half a year. I began kindergarten fresh again the next year, however a lot of the first graders remembered me from the year before. To kids that age, it was a bit confusing, but acceptable, everyone was in a new class, so it didn't matter who had really been in your class before, though it had been a question that I'd gotten asked several times throughout my schooling, the debate whether I had 'flunked' kindergarten or not.

Close to the end of my second grade year, I had taken several tests that my school had set only in front of me. They had taken me out of class and tested me on my own, in separate rooms, singling me out, for some reason unknown to me at the time. I did as I was told and completed every task they put in front of me. In third grade, I was invited to join 'Alert', which was our school's gifted program. I was excited for the opportunity, because I tended to get bored at times with some of the normal classroom work, so the challenge of something new intrigued me. It also didn't hurt that there were rumors that they were able to eat popcorn, drink soda in class, and they watched a lot of movies. To a nine year old, that sounded great. However, if I had known then, when I would experience in the coming years, I might have chosen not to participate. It wasn't that it wasn't fun, the things that we did were interesting and compelling, however misinterpreted by many of the teachers and other students involved in the school. Alert wasn't an extracurricular activity, it was a class that selected a few people from every grade that had IQ's higher than the average to go to a separate classroom for a few hours a week. The other kids and teachers thought that all we did in that class was have parties and get to skip out on normal class, however that wasn't the case. Most days we completed college level problem solving worksheets and prepared college level reports. Yes, we did get to eat popcorn and drink soda, but while we were formulating solutions for paperwork that was much, much higher than our level of education. I would find out though, that as much as we tried to tell others that it wasn't what they thought it was, even teachers participated in the shaming of the 'gifted students'. There were teachers that would refuse to give me the assignments I had missed while in Alert, they would tell me that because I missed it, I would have to get the information from another student, like I had 'skipped' their class or something, when in truth, I had only done what I was supposed to do. Both teachers and students treated us like we thought we were better than everyone else, which wasn't the case, by any means. In fact, to this day, my mother refuses to tell me the level my IQ tested to be then. Now, I'm sure, because of many, many reasons, some medical, it's likely not quite so high. I was in Alert up until my seventh grade year. It was in seventh grade that I had broken apart from what everyone 'wanted' me to do, to what I was going to do on my own.

My third grade year was one of the most difficult that I can remember in grade school. Right before school had started, I had broken my tailbone, which meant that most of the year that year, I had to sit on either a pillow or a medical donut. I chose a pillow, which ended up fodder for quite a few jokes as to why, though I tried not to let it bother me.

I was thirteen in seventh grade and anyone who remembers themselves or their children at thirteen knows that it is a turning point. Thirteen is that point between child and adult that you start to be your own person, feel more independent, and realize that there's more to the world than just the little bubble that your parents wanted to raise you in. Back then, of course, my mother restricted everything I did. Of course, she now had a first grader that, as I said before, tended to be a bit accident prone, so her attention was not always on me. My seventh grade year was the first time that I had ever gotten a grade lower than an A on anything. I remember, what it felt like to see that C- in Science, knowing it wasn't because I couldn't do it, but because I didn't want to. I chose not to turn in a lot of the homework, I chose to do just what I had to do to get by. Most importantly, I chose who I wanted to be that year, without even understanding the turning point I had made. That year was the first time anyone had ever heard me say a curse word, I began to try too hard to be like everyone else, which wasn't who I was meant to be. I tried to be what I thought my peers wanted, what I thought my peers would think was cool, the crazy thing about it was that a good majority of the time, it pushed people even further away. When I've tried to make others happy in my life, instead of myself, it always seemed to backfire on me, even to this day.

Eighth grade held a lot of changes for me, it was when one of my best friends in the world moved to town, it was when I had my first real boyfriend, my first kiss, our first school dance.

I am Murphy's Law

(NOVEL START [UNFINISHED] - 2016)

Have you ever thought of your life as if it were just a really drawn out movie, that just went beyond the credits? Maybe slightly broken up into parts, but one part just an extension of another, which is an extension of another, and on and on it goes from the beginning of life as you or I or we know it to the end. In my eyes, my life is a movie, it's just I'm the only one left watching. Sure, sometimes there are passerbys that watch for a while, eventually becoming bored or having something else to do, some stay longer than others, some interact with the actors or even become main characters in the plot line for a while... However, one way or another, most exit the stage eventually, some never to be seen of again, others popping up when a person least expects it, others just hanging around waiting to see where you're going with things. You see, as the writer of my own story, what most need to understand is, I have no idea where I'm going with this. That's right, I said it. I'm just walking out there on stage every day, waving to the crowd and rolling with it. Improv is great, right? Everybody loves it...well, except when you're kind of awkward about it, which I am.

Untitled

(NOVEL START [UNFINISHED] - 2014)

Chayne touched her finger to the top of the coin lightly, as she sat in the bright, sanitary conference room. When she had it positioned just right, she brought her other hand up and lightly thumped one side of the coin. The penny when skittering across the table on its side, coming to a halt still spinning on its edge. Chayne seemed to be watching it, but had other thoughts oscillating through her head right now.

She was brought from those thoughts suddenly when the door slammed open to her right, the boy whom entered was not a big surprise, considering what she knew of him. This kid couldn't keep from getting into trouble, it followed him around like his own personal storm cloud, raining and lightning, however most of the thunder came from him. There were rumors that his home-life was completely tragic. That was the only thing they were though. Rumors. No one truly knew the situation, they knew what they saw, and assumed they were right. He had never said that the rumors weren't true, but then he truly didn't speak much at all. Any class that Chayne had been in with him, he'd sat in the very back, seeming as if he was not paying attention. She had never seen him outside of school. He wasn't the type of person she would normally hang out with. The guy had light brown hair, floating down around his gaged ears. It always looked like it would be soft, as it had a slight gleam to it. His eyes were a grey-green, however they looked dark, almost black against his lightly tanned skin, eyelashes so dark that it almost seemed like he'd made them up to look that way. His face was lean, but with a mildly broad jawline, just like the rest of him lean, but mildly broad. His chin almost always seemed to have a thin stubble. His clothing was simple but clean; a white t-shirt, underneath a simple solid black, long-sleeved, button up shirt that fell at its hem about two inches above his knees. His jeans were a contrastingly light color, heavily torn at the knees, pooling down to his ankles and over his shoes. It seemed he had worn them so long that they had shredded themselves along the way, looking almost like thick, white hair growing from them on the floor behind him. Even his shoes were fairly plain, a small bit of bright red peeking from beneath the jeans that covered them, otherwise they were all black. The only thing he carried into the room was a denim jacket that he had draped over his arm, no books or notebooks, just a jacket. He made his way into the room, pulled on the rolling chair next to Chayne, slid it into the corner of the room completely opposite of the door, then dropped heavily into the seat. It didn't even seem that he'd noticed Chay was there, just as she tried to make it seem as if she hadn't noticed him either. When he had taken a seat, she finally reached across the table for her penny.

Just as she was leaning across the table, chest pressed flat on the surface, butt out in the air, in a very compromising position, another student walked in. With large eyes, Chay looked to her side to see whom it was, growing a bit of a blush from how he had caught her, 'getting her some Abe Lincoln'. She hoped it looked worse in her mind than it actually did to the kid, because in her head the scene looked fairly inappropriate.

The kid that walked in looked as if he should have been sent to the middle school conference room instead of the high school, which is one reason why Chay had been concerned for the way it had looked.. She gave the kid a half smile when he saw her look in his direction. His smile was large, which made him look even more childlike. He turned toward the hallway for a moment, telling someone behind him that 'this was the room'. 'Room for what?' Chey wondered. There were a few conference rooms, mostly used for teachers meetings and the like, but other than a single incident that stood out in her mind, she couldn't think of what either one of the boys had in common with her, so far. The kid walked in, being followed by a girl. The two couldn't have been more opposite. The boy almost looked like a porcelain doll, it seemed as if he hadn't gotten any sun since he was born. His hair was in the typical '1990's geek kid' haircut, parted to the side and combed toward the back. He wore a collared shirt and khaki pants, with brown dress shoes. He carried a stack of books so thick that Chay wasn't sure how he was actually holding it and not falling over or dropping them all over the floor. The girl behind him was African American; she had beautiful, sparkling, brown eyes; and her hair was pulled in a long, smooth braid that lay over her shoulder. She was wearing very little makeup, but she seemed to be one of those girls that didn't really need it. She had natural beauty. To Chay, she wasn't Miss America gorgeous, more like the pretty girl next door. The girl was thin, the type of person that Chay almost hated, one of those girls that could eat their weight in cupcakes every day for months and weigh less in the end than when she started. Her clothing was fairly simple, as well. She wore a light yellow t-shirt with a thin, baby blue, spring jacket; her jeans were clean with no holes or wear, the only embellishment some intentionally noticeable sand colored threading; and brown suede flats, their rounded toe barely peeking out from under her jeans. The only thing distinct about her was the very, very large bag with her. It looked almost like a gym bag, except from what Chay could see it hadn't a logo and it certainly wasn't their school color. This one was purple with black straps and their school colors were red and silver. Chay had always cringed and shook her head at calling it silver, everything that had their school colors on it was grey. There were easy ways to actually have silver for keepsakes; souvenirs; and school supplies , but not cheap ones, thus the school merely pretended everything was silver.

The two kids sat down directly across from Chayne, seeming to want to stay away from the boy in the corner. As they did so, they gave Chay and the boy nervous, questioning glances. It wasn't long before the younger looking boy spoke up and directed his questioning toward Chay, the only of the two that seemed comfortable with speaking, as it seemed.

"What's going on?" His voice was more forceful than his size and body would suggest. Not that he sounded as if he were trying to be angry or rude with Chay, but it was completely understandable to be on edge having been called into the small conference room by the school office, without advanced notice, with a bunch of peers that were basically unknowns to them. Hell, she was on edge herself. Chay shrugged.

"Dunno. When I walked in, I switched on the light, no one was in here." Chay took a quick glance at the boy in the corner. He had already put in earbuds and seemed to be sleeping with his head cradled in the corner behind him. This time she held her eyes on him for a few moments, almost searching him, feeling just as nervous with him sitting behind her as she did sitting in the conference room in general. The strings of the earbuds fell down to his jacket pocket, where Chay assumed there was an iPod or something. 'Probably stolen.' She thought to herself. The boy across from her went to reach his hand over the table to introduce himself, however stopped almost immediately, realizing that it wasn't going to reach.

"Steven." The boy made a hello motion, then gestured toward the girl to his left. "This is Violet. Her and I are in the same A. P. English class and were called in a few minutes ago." Steven made a motion toward the boy in the corner. "What about him? Do you know him? I don't believe I've seen him in any of my classes..." Steven seemed a bit full of himself. Even though he didn't actually say it, his tones suggested that he considered himself above the other boy, but Chay ignored it. Possibly this boy was just not much of a people person. Violet seemed to be a bit embarrassed that Steven had said that out loud, but didn't say anything. She, again completely opposite of her companion, seemed very quiet, almost shy, but it did seem as if she were taking mental notes of everything that was said.

"I'm Ch-..." Chay was cut off by the door opening once more, however this time it wasn't just another kid. Their principal also followed, closing the door behind him. This last student that entered really didn't need an introduction, as he was one of the school's star football players. Chay wasn't really sure what position he played, as she hadn't ever been much of a sports fan, but apparently he was very important to the team, from what she understood. Chay only knew the guy's last name. That's all she'd ever heard him called by, it's what his jersey said, and she'd never actually had a class with him. The principal walked toward the whiteboard and Freeman settled down in the seat beside her. Chayne's heart dumped from its original place in her chest to the floor in about two seconds flat when he sat down. Not only was Freeman important, he wasn't a bad looking guy. Freeman was mixed, his mother a very beautiful black woman who taught Chemistry in their school and his father was the city Medical Examiner and Coroner. Of course, having heard them called Dr. and Mrs. Freeman, Chay had no idea what their first names were either. The principal, on the other hand, was a bitter, angry, looking man, with features almost like a pepper-gray Col. Sanders. Everyone thought they knew why he was so angry. The man had two doctorates going to waste on merely a title. Not many were sure what his studied fields were or why he was not working in them, but it had always been a topic to avoid, as he was a bit touchy no matter who it seemed to be that asked. Now he couldn't get a better job than what he saw as 'playing babysitter to a bunch of angry, hormonal adolescents'. Chay was pretty sure that the man's grandchildren would likely be still paying off his student loans, considering the pay of a lowly high school principal versus the fields he'd likely studied. The older man stood at the whiteboard with his hands behind his back. Standing this way he looked a bit like a teapot; round in the middle, tiny at the top, and a handle in the back. His large round stomach protruded a bit out of his suit jacket while he stood this way. He looked over each student in the conference room with a glaring frown. Apparently Freeman and Hollisburg hadn't been having a good conversation as they'd walked together, if they had at all. When his eyes settled on the young man that had been in the corner, whom had started slowly rolling his way to the other side of the room, the frown disappeared and turned into a sharp sneer.

"Return the chair to its original location, Mr. Moore!" It was almost a growling yell that rippled out of the large man, jiggling his large belly like the Anti-Santa. The kid stood and moved the chair to its place, more casually than most would have after such a yell, then plopped down in it, without looking at the man, nor hanging his head. 'Mr. Moore', as the principal had called him, seemed as if he had something to prove, and not just to Dr.Hollisburg, but to the world in general. The principal, began to walk around the table, still in the same teapot position, but this time slightly forward, seeming as if he were pouring himself out. Chay might have smiled or laughed at the thought of him pouring himself out, if Dr. Hollisburg wasn't so eerily silent. When he reached the whiteboard, having not looked at anyone or anything except the floor, he looked toward the table of adolescents. "All of you should know why you're here. There should be no need for me to remind you. Some of you..." He looked toward Freeman, Chay, and Moore, then toward Steven and Violet. "...have seen me more than others." He paused again, before continuing. "However, this school system would like to see you five succeed." He paused again, his face twisting as if he'd just tasted something disgusting, however continued almost as if he were reading from a script. "According to the nationwide standardized tests, along with your school records, and...police records." His eyes moved toward Moore, whom rolled his eyes, then back to all five of them. "You five qualify to have full scholarships, through the federal government to attend the F. A. West Program's Academy for troubled teens." Chay could tell that the last part made him want to giggle and dance in hopes that the five's parents would sign the release. Dr. Hollisburg reached his right hand into the inside pocket of his jacket and pulled out a few envelopes and for the last time he walked around the table, placing an envelope in front of each kid. The envelopes were all sealed and each had a specific name on it. When the principal reached Moore, he didn't place an envelope in front of him. "...yours has already been mailed to your parents...and your probation officer." Moore got up forcefully, sending the chair rolling behind him, making it slam against the wall.

"You piece of shit!" Moore shouted and pointed toward the KFC spokesman look-alike. "You'll get yours, you prick son of a bitch...you'll get yours!" Moore left the room, slamming the door behind him. Chay made a mental note about the fact that Moore had only pointed at the man, instead of a certain gesture that she almost expected from him. What the young man had said, didn't seem to be marked this time with anger and rebellion, as much as it seemed to have upset and scared him, his voice seeming to have almost cracked when he shouted it. Dr. Hollisburg, a smug smile painted over his face, looked back toward the other teens.

"Well now, if there isn't any other questions, children...I

have a school to run. You're dismissed." The principal walked slowly to the door, whistling 'Happy Trails to You' as he walked through the door, closing it behind him.

After the good doctor left, the four remaining sat for a few moments in complete silence. It was Steven and Violet that got up to leave first. Surely they were walking back to their Advanced Placement classes. They left Chayne wondering what they must have done to have put themselves in this sort of situation.

She looked toward Freeman, whom was still staring at the name on the envelope. Vince. His name was Vince Freeman. He seemed lost in his thoughts. He looked sad and confused, but somehow he also seemed to understand at the same time. He looked like he needed someone to talk to.

"Are you going to go?" Chay asked him, still looking at her envelope and placing it flat on the table. She was stalling, she wasn't really in a rush to go to Biology, the smell of the lab always made her stomach do backflips. It didn't help that they had scheduled her Biology directly after lunch. Nothing makes you toss your cookies like carving a fetal pig after eating a pork chop for lunch. Vince jumped when he heard her voice, as if he had no idea there was still anyone in the room, pulling his eyes reluctantly from the envelope to Chayne.

"I dunno, you?" His outer appearance displayed a causal, strong disposition, yet his eyes said something else. There was a softness to them, like teddy bear eyes or the eyes of a puppy. "Probably deserve it. Need to read through it. Didn't seem we like we had much of a choice, though." He glanced toward the door, then back at his envelope. "I gotta go, talk this out with coach and…" He dropped what he was saying, as if something he said had just pulled him into thought. After a moment, his gaze snapped up, as if the mask of the popular football player was thrust back on him, and he gave her a forced half smile, in a single obvious motion, he tried to get a peek of her name over the top of her envelope. "See ya around, Chayne." Except he pronounced it, 'Chain' instead of 'Shane'. Before she could correct him though, he was through the door.

Chayne took a deep breath, looking back down at the name on her own envelope. It was her parent's fault that everyone called her Chain, having been born in the post hip-hop generation, everyone wanted to name their kid something 'different'. At this point, Chay would have just settled for being average. Then maybe she wouldn't be in this situation. She got up slowly, pushing her chair in gently behind her. Chay folded the letter in half and placed it in her jacket pocket. Chay knew why she would likely be heading off to the other school and she didn't doubt the justice of it, karma always comes back to you...usually ten fold.

Seph couldn't believe the audacity of that son of a bitch. He pulled an olive green canvas bag from his locker, stuffing several books, notebooks, and papers into it, before slamming it closed. That prick had had it out for Seph since he'd moved into the school system a couple of years ago. Always painted the bad kid, but never a reason why. There were kids that could get away with murder and then there were kids like Seph. The guy whom they branded the troublemaker, the bad kid, the rebel before they even knew a single thing about him other than the way things appeared to be from the outside. As he walked through the heavy metal doors, he pulled his phone from his pocket. One-thirty. It wouldn't take him long to get home, but he wasn't sure if the mail would be there yet. He hoped so. That damn letter was just another nail in the coffin that the principal was trying to build for him. Seph walked down the sidewalk slowly and after a few blocks, he met the mailman at the door. He nodded his thanks to the mailman, quietly and deliberately he stepped toward the door of the house, making sure to step on the boards of the porch that he knew wouldn't make a sound. His mom would be sleeping right now and he didn't want to wake her. He quickly thumbed through the mail until he found the letter marked 'to the parents of' and quickly slid it into his back pocket. He turned back toward the street, tossed the rest of the mail back into the mailbox, and walked away from the house. It wouldn't be long before he reached his destination, Gateway Park. He needed some time to think.

Gateway Park was many things, it was in the center of town, the hub of socialization for men, women, and children children; with basically something for everyone. However, that wasn't the reason he came here. He walked slowly along the sidewalk, holding onto the strap of his backpack, eyes moving around, taking everything in as he walked. As he passed the playground, he watched the giggling toddlers too young for grade school, mothers and fathers smiling and laughing, or babysitters sitting alongside on the park benches, chatting amongst themselves, all of which made a smile light up his face. He passed them with envy, it had been a long time since he'd felt the true joy that those people had at the moment, their togetherness. His eyes turned forward, not wanting to pull away from the happy scene. He'd learned early on after moving to this town, that sitting along side of the family play area, and watching all the fun they were having seemed creepy to some. He'd been warned more than once to take a hike, there it was again, the assumption that he was a bad kid. The park just reminded him of once upon a time when things in life weren't so broken, when he was too young to understand that sometimes life just isn't fair. Sometimes life wants to rip everything you have from you and laugh in your face for mourning the loss of that happiness and innocence. It's called being a teenager, the hard road that must be traveled in order to become an adult. It's the age that you realize that there really are monsters out there, they just aren't green and scaly. They're all around you, disguised as 'normal' people, but as heartless and evil as any demon or monster that you'd ever heard about when you were young.

Seph passed the skatepark and basketball courts fairly quickly, considering there weren't many kids there during school hours and those that were there, he'd found out early on that not only didn't he fit in, he didn't really want to. His sanctuary wasn't far from the courts, within a small forgotten corner of the park. Since he'd moved to town, he'd explored every bit of the park, not only for something to do, but for somewhere to get away.

The concrete tube was mostly camouflaged with years of overgrowth in the little wooded oasis. It was apparent that it hadn't actually been used in years, likely abandoned for a newer, better water drainage system. Seph pulled the curtain of ivy away from the entrance of the tube, having kept them growing to maintain the disguise. When inside he sat down and leaned back against the cold concrete and just took a breath, a long hard sigh that seemed to say everything he felt without speaking a single word. It had been a long hard couple of years and it was beginning to wear on him. His mother, the divorce, moving and leaving everything and everyone behind that he once knew. The worst part about it was, if it had been that tough on him, it had been even worse on his mother. She was the reason he didn't want to go home. He didn't want to face her if his probation officer had called her, and he certainly didn't want to give her the letter in his back pocket if it had anything negative to say about him. She had been through enough the last couple of years, without thinking her son was going to be forced to go to some prison camp for bad kids. To add to the fact, it wouldn't be likely that the probation officer would give her the news in any way but a negative sort. Seph needed more information about the subject so that he would be able to twist it in a way that his mother could handle it. If he was going to have to go to this school or organization or program, whatever it was, he needed a way to tell his mother that it could be a good thing, rather than pile on more bad news for her. They'd both had a lot more bad news than they could handle for a while.

Seph reached into his backpack and pulled out a clip on reading light and affixed it to a bolt protruding out of the concrete, pulling the letter from his back pocket, and taking another look at it. 'To the Parents of Joseph A. Moore', address, stamp, strangely though there wasn't a return address. The envelope was thin, business stock, and the lazy kind that you just pull the tab and it already has the glue there for you, not the kind that you have to lick. No one wants to do things the long way anymore, everyone has to have a shortcut. It didn't seem heavy like an acceptance letter from a college would be, it seemed as if it likely only had a single piece of paper or two inside, possibly a brochure.

Seph reached into his right pocket, pulling out his pocket knife, and with a flick of his wrist proceeded to slice the top crease of the envelope, opening it. By basically using muscle memory alone, he closed the knife and slid it back into his pocket, as he pulled out the information from the envelope. Now using both hands, he unfolded the two papers inside. He looked at both papers a few times, sat them down on his lap, he picked the envelope back up to make sure he hadn't missed something. Seph was confused, this wasn't what he had expected at all. He folded the papers back up, slid them back in the envelope, then squished them into his bag. He needed some time to think on what the contents of the letter meant and if it might mean something more to his mother or there had been something else coming with this paperwork that he'd already missed or was on it's way. All of these options swirled around in his mind, as he stared blankly at the concrete in front of him. He wondered if the others had received the same thing or something different. He was curious, but likely not curious enough to want to see those stuck up assholes again, was he? He pulled his earbuds out of his pocket, the cord had never been attached to anything, but people will say anything when they think that no one is listening. He actually plugged the earbuds into his phone, starting a music app. He only put the left side in, allowing him to hear if anyone or anything might come near. No one ever had, but one couldn't be too careful sometimes. It wasn't long before Seph drifted off to sleep, lost in his own thoughts, and concerns.

2

Chayne slammed the locker door, after having taken all of her things from it, lifting her backpack to her shoulder. It was her last day in public school and she gave her awaiting friends looks of sorrow, as she hugged them for what felt like the last time ever. She could feel the tears welling up in her eyes, as she held tightly to the two girls for a few moments, before she let go. Slowly parting from each other, all three girls seemed to be slightly weepy.

"We'll still see each other on birthdays and major holidays." One of the two girls spoke optimistically. Chayne who was still almost ready to cry, began a light laughter. That was just like Heather to think on the 'bright side' of things. Chayne would miss these days, the days when the three of them roamed the halls together in their small little pack. Adults these days liked to think that there were no cliques these days, that everyone was friends with everyone else; there were no bullies, no mean girls, no nerds, no jocks, no slackers...however, that's just the way it seemed on the outside. Internally there was still that same social hierarchy, it was merely focused through digital ways now, instead of through physical interaction. In fact, it was easier these days to maintain social status, as you didn't have to be afraid to say anything anymore, another girl could pick on you from afar, and not have another care in the world after that. Chanye knew how that felt all too well and in some ways she was glad she was leaving this place.

The mixed feelings she felt as she walked to the exit of the building with the two girls grew. They had been her best friends since they had started grade school together and now she was leaving them. She was leaving them for the unknown, before she ever thought she would be. They had all planned things out in middle school together, how they would all go to the same college, move to the same town, marry best friends, and raise all their children together, with a cat and a dog, and a white picket fence... Now, all those dreams seemed to fade into nothingness right before her eyes, in this very moment. Of course, the way she remembered it after that day had always been much more dramatic than it actually was. To her she was being ripped from her life, everything she knew. Torn from her whole world to join a new unknown, venture out into a new frontier. Afterall, it would be a new school, with mostly new people, a boarding school nonetheless, something she'd never experienced before in her entire life. She had no idea that there were actually still boarding schools in existence, she'd thought such a primitive notion went out of fashion with polos and khaki pants. Though, her parents weren't millionaires, merely middle, working class individuals, so how would she know what kind of schools rich kids went to these days. The 'richest kids' in her school had always turned their noses up at her, even though it was likely they weren't any richer than she, their parents merely spent more money on them and their 'appearance' to be so. Chayne didn't truly care what position she held within the social hierarchy, however she did care that she was leaving her only friends behind. What, was she supposed to be friends with Steven and Violet, the geek twins? Or Vince, the football player that had barely even spoken to her before now? She'd decided the day she'd walked into the conference room that there was no way she was getting any closer to the only other option. Rumor was that he was a criminal that had to transfer because he'd been kicked out of every other school in the area, she wasn't about to even try to befriend someone like that, even thinking about it gave her the creeps.

With a heavy heart and a loud thud, she tossed her backpack in the back seat of her mom's SUV and gave her friends one last wave. She wasn't sure when she would see them again. She had no idea what her new schedule would be like, she hadn't even been to this new school just yet. Her parents had been invited for a preliminary tour, but they had left her behind, considering the 'accident' that led her to be in this situation and the reason she was going, her fate was being decided for her at the moment.

THE SEMI-CURRENT

(Works 2017 to Now)

There Was a Time

(POETRY - 2019 - WRITTEN FOR MY HUSBAND, JEREMEY)

There was a time…
When I thought I had to act below average to fit in.
There was a time…
When those around me convinced me I didn't matter and I wasn't good enough.
There was a time…
When I thought being different was a bad thing.
There was a time…
When I let people walk on me and use me because I so desperately needed a connection.
There was a time…
Where I felt alone and sad, even in a room full of 'friends'.
There was a time…
When I felt like I would only ever be a burden to those I love.
There was a time…
Where I cried more than I smiled.
There was a time…
When I was convinced that real love did not exist.
There was a time…
When I thought that all of this was okay.
Now I know…
That my uniqueness, intelligence, and talents are good things.
Now I know…

That I am good enough, in fact, I'm pretty great for many reasons.
Now I know...
My eccentricity is one of my best features.
Now I know...
I don't deserve to be treated badly or used, I deserve so much more in life than a lot of people offer me.
Now I know...
I'm not alone, so many wonderful people care, genuinely want me in their life, and appreciate me for who I am.
Now I know...
I will always be a blessing to the people in my life that matter.
Now I know...
I have so many reasons to smile.
Now I know...
What love actually is and what it really means.
Now I know...
That it wasn't okay, it never was.
I know all of these things because of you. You are my rock, my lantern, my laughter, my smile, my joy, my wake up call...
You are the reason for my happiness in a world full of darkness.
Thank you.

Remember, Remember the 18th of December

(POETRY - 2020 - WRITTEN FOR OUR NATION)

"Remember, remember the 18th of December...
When once we thought our darkest days,
Forever would they render.
Our people, hurting and in despair
Both sides yelling, it isn't fair!
For months both sides felt unheard,
For months they felt misunderstood,
We saw each other's views absurd,
Trying to save each other, if we could.
Friends and families broke apart,
Years of connections shattered.
Mothers and children with broken hearts,
Each feeling as if their opinions were all that mattered.
Four years of turmoil, maybe more,
Until both sides, had hit the floor.
We did our part, felt truth would prevail,
Until seven states seemed to 'check the mail'.
Conditioned to believe whatever we're told,
The streets to destruction, for some, are paved with gold.
Our people, they all had good intentions,
Unfortunately, conflict has fallout they sometimes fail to mention.
Our nation divided by political position,

Almost as if both sides were on a mission.
Isolated more by a mysterious illness,
This only fueled the fires and clinched the fists.
But as our people, they worried alone,
The wheels had been moving more than they'd known.
You see, behind the scenes they'd seen all along,
There were far too many involved doing wrong.
They dug through the files and compiled some reports,
A packet of evidence on all the cohorts.
Maybe the most strategic plan the world had ever seen,
If you're on their side, you'd better be watching your queen.
In chess, all moves are made for checkmate,
But by the time some realize what's going on it might be too late.
Corruption won't last for long in our lands,
Not as long as our nation, our patriots, and our faith in our country still stands.
Remember, remember the 18th of December..."

We Immortals

(NOVEL START [UNFINISHED - FUTURE POSSIBLE] - 2017)

"How to describe those days to someone who hadn't experienced them, in a way that hadn't already been written in some sort of apocalyptic science fiction novel? There are no words that can fully express the true evils that the human condition is capable of when threatened with extinction...extinction of a way of life, of moral values, of knowledge...the primal instinct overpowering human civilization. Everything is a cycle, history repeats itself, eventually everything comes back around and in these, the days once more of nomads, hunters, and monsters, one can not be too careful. This wasn't in the long term plan, it wasn't even in a risk profile, it was as if it conquered us overnight, crept up while we weren't looking and enveloped us, even though we, as a species, had been the full causality. The intellects of the world should have seen it, they should have been able to predict the collapse before it was too late, but as distracted by shiny things as we had all become, we reveled in the 'immortality' of our species, the feeling that we were indestructible, bulletproof, and entitled. We fell because of our own greed, not truly for the material, as much as for life itself. That greed is what finally took us in the end. It wasn't an alien race, it wasn't a zombie infection...we took ourselves down." - Luc Maddox [Survivor, 2026]

[This is a work of fiction and not meant to be taken any other way. Though some instances may be based on fact, this is not intended to be a prediction of the future, but is intended to warn those who might be ignorant of circumstances, to think about the choices they make in their own futures. Be warned of the possibilities, question the world, but contribute to it as well...hope for the best and prepare for the worst. Always.]

Chapter 1

Part One- The Blissful Undead

It was hard for most to see back then, face buried in a phone or a book or always looking for the next place to be, the next thing to do, the next thing to see or feel. The end of days didn't come with one single act, it came with a ladder of chaos that none could see building until all of the weight was on top and it came crashing down. We the self proclaimed governing race of the world, the gods of our own domain...the cancer of our own planet, growing and growing until we amassed overwhelming capacity at an alarming rate, uncaring as to what we consumed or destroyed. Life, as we knew it, was good back then. That was all we cared about. As long as our own tiny world remained in tact, we each, as individuals, created a society of the heartless. Isn't that truly what a zombie is? A creature continuing life, dulled of senses, heartless, only a mind to guide them from the destruction of one individual to the next. For you see, our zombies came before the apocalypse, not after, and it was the zombies that in the end were the first to be exterminated. However, in the beginning, many of those zombies were the most dangerous of all.

However, let us back up a bit further, all the way back to a year before the lights went out and networks collapsed. I get ahead of myself too far and the end will be here before we know it, not the true end, but it very well could be eventually, whereas we may never build ourselves back to what we once were. There are some things that need to be noted before I get into the actual story itself, considering a stage needs to be set, the description of that time accurately recorded for future generations, whether they ignore like we did or take heed, someone needs to say it. Sometimes, the world as I once knew it, seems like a faded memory of an almost completely forgotten dream. The world where a person was told when they were a child that they could grow up and be anything they wanted to be, because we were a free country where you could follow your dreams. However, in those days, the days I grew up in, all the dreams had been dreamed, all the words had been spoken, all the possible outcomes of all of the stories already told, nothing was original any longer, because someone had already considered it before. That was the mind frame of the masses, so to those in normal everyday civilization, the possibility of greatness was highly improbable, so much so that most faith and hope had already been lost. True faith and hope, not the type they sell you in a church or a political agenda preaches, the type that can only be felt deep down in one's soul, because it has to be, because everything else has been stripped away layer by layer. We had been built up too much to see that, padded with so much political correctness that encircled us in a bubble. A bubble that, before the collapse, allowed us to get back up and running whenever we stumbled. However, the day we fell that bubble popped so loudly that it was heard around the world and reverberated into the minds, bodies, and souls of each individual and brought them to their knees.

You see, it wasn't just one country. It hadn't only been us that had been falling apart, like we had once thought. The truly sad part was that we chose not to see it, we chose to be ignorant, we complained about how the world was falling apart, how people's lives had changed for the worse, how the day was so miserable for everyone, but then sat complacent. We didn't look outside of our own window, at our proverbial neighbor's house that was also going down in flames, because we had started our own fires. The internet had become a way of escape, a way to divert our attention from the world that was crumbling around us. The internet was cat videos and memes and little images with inspiring phrases on them, keeping us from having to look at the cold hard truth that our world was decaying, as we kept on watching what was on the screen in front of us.

Looking back it's almost unimaginable that we'd ignored it for so long, pushed away the warning signs like that fly that bugs you while you're busy working on something you deem 'important'. In a way, nothing within those days seems important anymore, other than for purposes of records sake, for historical reasons to rectify our future or to justify our past. We will never listen though. We will never learn. We as a species have been destroying ourselves since the beginning of time, in history books that likely no one will ever see, a past that we were all once taught, but it's not likely anyone will ever read again. As we considered ourselves and our creations immortal, we found ways of removing what we saw as clutter and 'the old ways', things that we saw as replaceable and unnecessary. After all, where are the eBooks now that the internet no longer exists? What good is your cell phone or your tablet, when there is no working outlet to plug into? It can't be eaten, it can't be traded, it is useless and cold and there is nothing about it worth saving. The comfortable lifestyle is a thing of the past. Society took what had been built for granted, wanting more and more for less and less, until there was nothing left to give.

At the time, they blamed the Millennials, those that grew up around the turn of the century. However, it wasn't really their fault. Of course, they ruled the world when everything finally came to a crashing halt, they were the ones to have pushed it over the edge, but they didn't cause it completely. This had been building since the dawn of a new era, the era of technology, the era where we became our own gods. Not that I have ever been a religious person, in general, however when one only has faith in himself and not that of anyone else around him or believes that nothing is above him, that man no longer has anything to fear, nothing that holds much importance, and nothing to do with anything beyond himself. This began with the first machines.

The first machines were created as tools, tools to help us work harder and more efficiently. These tools were to allow us to work a full day and come home to enjoy our families, allow our children to enjoy being a child and not have to work alongside us in whatever factory, because someone along the way deemed a child unfit to do the work that an adult does. Which, to an extent is a truth, however then someone deemed that they should sit in generalized education every day, the unspoken truth to this was to keep them busy until they were of working age, then place them where they would be most useful. Of course, that was in the beginning. Somewhere along the way, our race got this crazy idea that a person could choose their designation. The idea that 'if you work really hard in school and get good marks, you can go on to more school and they will teach you how to do something that doesn't come naturally to you'. That was the idea anyway, unfortunately it backfired. When these children grew up and either hated their life for choosing a designation that wasn't what they were meant to do or figured out that they had wasted so much of their life working toward something that was never going to happen, they became bitter and angry. People had the freedoms to hate their station in life, by now they had the means of communications with the invention of the telephone, the radio, and eventually the television, to convey that unrest.

Communications began to soar and the ideals and importance of family and marriage began to break, as one man, one woman, found someone else, because they thought if they changed partners or changed places they could change that unrest in their lives. However, from that came more unrest, which was passed on to their children and their children's children, until at some point in time the reason for that anger had been completely lost. It was not that it wasn't remembered in books and on the internet, it was that no one truly remembered what actually created that unrest in the first place. No one remembered what it felt like to actually feel the injustices that truly were in the world and with actual injustice, mostly eradicated, those who were still angry from generations of that turmoil, found new things to be angry with. Whether those things were justified was up to which side of the fence you were on, however, the truth was that those who cried of the injustices of the world, had truly never faced actual oppression. They could read about it in history, but the human being always believes that his situation is worse than the next man, without truly asking the next man what he is going through. It is the human condition to be unsatisfied, to want more from life...however, it was the current condition after the millennium to feel as if one deserved more merely because of their existence. Abortion rates ran rampant and apparently it was considered that if a person survived the womb, freedom meant that they were entitled to whatever they wished without putting in the actual effort to get it. Now, it is understandable the want for survival, all creatures in life have want for survival. However, if a tiger has need for food, it does not sit there and wait until the food comes to him, he hunts for it, chases it, takes it down, and claims it for himself. A tiger is not entitled to his dinner, any moreso than a human being. Yes, feed the children, take care of the weak, the sick, the elderly, and the dying. However in the world we lived in, the beggars were able bodied enough to create chaos, in a world that had already begun to die.

It was in these times that we were not truly living, we were existing. Life requires work and sacrifice, it requires moving forward and creating, building and sustaining. We had stalled. We were at a stalemate. People did not want to grow up with a dream, their dream was to never grow up, to be a child for the rest of their lives and demand that the world take care of them while they chose to stay home and play. The more societies that became this way, the more the world began to fall, with the internet now mainstream, these social 'injustices' grew state to state, nation to nation, until our entire world was comprised of those who could not understand why their neighbor had 'something better', but refused to see the work that had been put into achieving that 'something better'.

Instead of working harder to achieve such goals in their life, they chose to burn their neighbor's house down out of jealousy, and the government which had taken a turn for the worse, feeling it was their job to appease the public and not control it, allowed the fires as a statement of the freedoms of our nation. Of course, this is something of a metaphor, the fires didn't truly start before the actual fall, however injustice was rampant, it merely wasn't seen as society viewed it. In these days, the world of our ancestors had been turned upside down. Criminals were painted as martyrs, peacekeepers shown as devils, the individual seen as a hateful creature out to destroy one another, but only in the eyes of those next to him. Robbers were compensated for their injuries when men protected their families from invasion of their homes. The homeowners went to jail, the robbers made more money in lawsuits than they might have even gotten out of anything they had stolen. Men stood up for causes that only existed out of persistence of those involved to maintain the imagery and ideals they claimed to be against. Society worked against the goals they said they stood for and could not see beyond their own front yard, though with information everywhere, claimed to know what life and the world was about more than any other. This generation had created a generation of Internet Experts, whose main goal was to believe that they knew better than the next person, though they had no reasoning other than they watched the news or the read an article on the internet to back it up. Recorded history was ignored for what someone new claimed to know about someone else during the time history was written; when truly how could anyone in this age know anything about what had happened one hundred and fifty or two hundred years ago? Rumors spread were believed more than factual information, guilty until proven innocent, bad until proven good. The soft minded retreated to their safe places, out of harm of the spoken word or what they deemed damaged about life. The fight in the human race was left to the ill-informed and the most savage among us, those who merely enjoyed the fight because they could personally gain from it and not how society as a whole would prosper.

It was these creatures, those savages that would eventually become the monsters in my story, determined to only consume, uncaring as to what or whom fell within their path, these were the creatures that eventually caused the lights to go out...

Part Two - The Sheep and the Wolves

The end, as I said, came quickly. Not as quickly as it feels now though, but then because the aftermath is still ongoing and progressing, it's hard to truly know when 'the end' finally finished and 'the aftermath' began, it's almost as if the two blended together to some extent.

Pre-downfall, I considered myself a visionary, a progressed individual, someone who rejected societal norms, and to an extent I was. Unfortunately, life had given me a hand of bad luck and at that point in time; I was living with my mother, her new husband, my younger brother, two cats, and a dog. Life simply was. My brother was what I considered a Millennial, having been born just before the turn of the millennium. The existential definition of a hipster. I had been out, done things in the world, then upon failing had returned to my mother's roof to pick up the broken pieces of my shattered life. My brother had never left. He preached his injustice from the rooftops, while still living in our mother's house, without rectifying the actual injustices he contributed to society. After the fall, my brother made his choice, after which I didn't see him for years. Yet again, I'm getting ahead of myself.

At that time, I was 35. I was recovering from a divorce that had left me not only broken and downhearted, but also just plain broke. She'd taken me for everything. Apparently, I had driven her to infidelity due to the consummation of my life by my job, a job that left little time for her. Closer to fact was that along with my full time job and writing in my downtime, she chose to watch television and sit on the phone that I provided for her. She had a lot of free time on her hands. While I worked to afford our bills, apparently Rafael, the man who cleaned the neighbor's pool, saw that she didn't have quite enough to do. I hope they're happy wherever they are, I'm sure they didn't last long with the way of the world now.

When I had moved back home, I still worked, but I also focused on my writing, thinking that eventually I'd end up being the next Hemingway, of course choosing to ignore the fact that no one actually read books anymore. Society could just watch the movie, they didn't need to use their minds, when a producer would come along and find the next Harry Potter and put it on the big screen. I found it funny how much difference a period of five years made, back then. The difference of opinion between my brother and I, I fought my battles through putting writing to a page, he fought his battles by picking fights through a computer screen. I'm not going to lie, I had Facebook as well, and if I saw something worth fighting for, I would mention my strong opinions to the masses, however I left most things alone. In the age of technology, I was outnumbered. I could see what was going on, sitting back and watching, I knew something was coming, just not exactly what or how it would begin. I could see the unrest building, but being a single person and not of power or influence, all I could do was watch things fall apart. My mother and her douche-bag of a new husband watched the news and did their part in conventional ways; voting, going to church, praying, volunteering, things that they had always known to help in the past. However, this was not the past and as far as I was concerned, any god that might have existed at one point in time was either dead or had abandoned us for a creation that might be more worthy of such a supreme being. Everything my parents knew was outdated and though they liked to think that they were caught up with the current times because they had smartphones and Facebook, they had no idea what the world really was now. They saw happenings as they did from a biased media, a news channel that they thought was bringing them things as they were, but had no idea that the media was so corrupt. They expected the same news to be on every channel, expected every channel to say the same things, unknowing that each channel spun the truth so that their viewers would hear things as they wanted them to hear, to further someone else's agenda. By that time, I had mainly stopped watching the news. To an extent, I kept an eye out for what was happening in the world, but I couldn't rely on the words of the broadcasters, I had to rely on what my mind and heart told me and what they had to say wasn't good.

I purchased a pistol. I tried to store supplies, but unknowing as to when whatever would happen things merely went out of date and I would have to waste and replace. It didn't make much sense to hoard things that would ultimately not be useful if something were to happen. I said nothing to my current household, what good would it do to be caught in a sanitarium for 'paranoid and delusional' thoughts? I kept most things to myself in those days, though I still tried to prepare for anything. It wasn't delusion, it was survival instinct, something that, at that time, most of society had lost.

I realize that up until this point, I have discussed a lot of what might have been personal opinion. I have talked about how I considered history and the world, I have spoke of what I've seen as if it were such times of great unrest...and it was, but only selectively so. The media spun webs of the righteous rioters on one channel and the dangerous looters on another, it was hard to understand where the truth really lie, because our information was coming from the most ignorant among us. Reporters that filmed for the television crews chose the person they thought might give them the most entertaining information, which was generally the most ill-educated and outlandish person they could find in the group. These things happened on and off for years. I focused mainly on my own world, trying to shut out the influences of the outside world, as if somehow that might make everything go away. As if somehow, if I didn't see it, if I didn't know about it it didn't exist and wouldn't overflow into the little place in the world that I had built for myself.

Though these were the days that led up to the fall, I don't count these within the fall itself, because as I said, it had been building, in my opinion, since before I was born. The fall itself began at the end of the year 2019. To be honest, as I also said, I am not sure when it truly ended and the aftermath of that fall began, however, I do know that it came on swiftly and within a few months time a third of our population had been wiped out. The wolves had taken down the sheep in herds and what sheep they didn't take down, became allied with them, not true wolves, but under their protection for later elimination or use. It wasn't exactly how science fiction had portrayed the apocalypse as going, but from the inside looking out, it seemed a fairly close depiction at the time.

Let me also make something understood, these first two parts, this first chapter, every word within it, is based on personal experience and my thoughts at the time. There are small pieces of factual information, based on my own experiences, but a majority is merely retention on what my own mind went through as these things occurred. I am sure later in this account of information, I will add more thoughts and action as I recount the way things occurred, as I perceived them to have happened. Every word I write, which may never be read by another person, is the truth as I have seen it and everything to come, is what happened from my perception. The perception of another might have been much different and in the hopes that a society may rise once again, it is my desire to eventually compare those interactions to see the way others might have experienced the world as it fell. That, in itself, would be the greatest apocalypse movie of all time. This first chapter is merely a basis to begin, a starting of point, if you will. This chapter is a look at who I am and how I perceive things that have happened, the next few will be the experiences that led me to those conclusions. The next few chapters will be about the fall itself, the aftermath of such, and the desolation of what is now reality. This paper, these notebooks, this package of pens that I found in a looted store, things that no one wanted, but are now so precious to me, these are my testaments that I will leave before the wolves might catch up to me. I will carry them with me as I travel and someday hope that someone might find them useful. I am not afraid of the wolves, though I am not one myself, neither am I a sheep. Through these trials and tribulations, I have stood, not as a man, as humanity has outlived its rule...but as a sheepdog.

Chapter 2

Part One - Mainstream Media and Defense against the Times

I was working the night the network fell. The night the electricity went out and the backup generators came on. They didn't last, of course, not as long as I wished they had, though it wouldn't have mattered. There weren't many in the end to have need for them. The glass doors of the store should have been bulletproof. They weren't of course, because at that time, no business presumed they would get robbed and looted. However, in the beginning, the afraid masses flooded to the stores to get supplies for what they thought might be over soon. Chaos ensued and though law and order tried to be kept, it wasn't the lawful citizen that was armed, it was the lawless. The monsters, as I would later call them...not to be confused with the wolves, which we will get into later, because I have many designations during these times, but the monsters and the sheep were the first to fight it out, the first to show themselves during these times. When the first part of the fall began to shift, there weren't many of this first round of sheep left alive.

As things began to die down, I realized I'd kept myself hidden in the store for three days. The analog watch on my wrist had counted them for me and I'd kept track as I could hear the anarchy just beyond my chosen hiding place. However, after these three days, the world became quiet. The screams, gunshots, and panic seemed to be over and what felt like a nightmare, I thought was now finished. Unfortunately, what I didn't realize was that my own apocalypse had only just begun.

I hadn't eaten anything in those days I'd been hidden and had barely thought to grab the closest available hydration I could, which had been a bottle of Gatorade. With the electrolytes that it provided, it had probably been a fairly good choice in the heat of the moment. Certainly better than a two liter of soda that, had I been hidden for longer, could have likely killed me instead.

What remained in the store, as I walked through isle after isle, seemed almost humorous to me, things that we'd wanted before, but didn't even matter now. I even remember having kicked a fallen bean bag chair out of my way, at one point. It wasn't until I reached the more survival based areas that I actually laid eyes on the collateral damage of what had taken place. It was in that moment that all five of my senses glazed over, as I stared out into a sea of fallen sheep for the first time. It wouldn't be the last, but I will always remember it, as it had been the moment when I had realized that everything I'd ever known to be, no longer existed.

I had stood there for what had been only moments, but seemed like days, my glazed eyes not truly wanting to see, but unable to pull away. I brought my hand to my mouth, not only because I could feel the bile rising from my gut, but also to make sure that what my eyes saw before me was real and I wasn't dreaming. I'd known what terrors were likely happening, but, as I'd been hiding, I'd tried to shut it out as if someone had left the tv on too loud. I'd tried to be immune to what had went on, as if it wasn't real...and it was within this moment that everything became too real.

I could tell that some had been lying there since the beginning, days old dead, eyes glazed over with that white that they try to portray in the movies, but it's still not quite the same as in person. The lifelessness is almost unbearable, especially when a person looks out upon body after body, so many dead in so many different ways. I had walked into hell, only it wasn't hot or on fire, it was in the grocery section of a supercenter. Any craving for food I'd had within that moment, had been lost due to the threat of vomiting that still hung heavy in my throat. Almost soundlessly, I made my way back to sporting goods. I had no idea what kind of individuals might still be lingering in the large store and I have never been a fool. Most of the department had been cleaned out, but I grabbed what I could. The case to the guns had been broken, nothing was left. All of the knives that had been on display were gone, however, with my experience in the store, I knew where they kept extra stock.

At this moment, it was the pistol that I had bought that I thought of. Useless. I had some ammunition saved, but what good is a pistol when you run out of bullets? Hopefully my family had thought to use it, if they had needed it. I had been thinking of them the entire time I'd been trapped here. It would have come as a shock to my parents. My brother, who knew what he might have done in this scenario. He had love for his family, but at times, one wondered if his love for himself overpowered familial loyalty.

I grabbed a sports bag and threw anything into it that I could find left that I might need, less food, because I couldn't go back to that aisle again, at least not at this time anyway. As I was heading back to storage, it was then that I found Geary.

I wouldn't know his name for quite some time, but in the beginning it didn't really make much difference, calling him 'kid' worked just as well. Hiding amongst the boxes, shocked and afraid of the man with the bag that stared down at him, the boy couldn't have been more than twelve. The kid didn't look at all suited to the situation, slightly overweight and pale, as if he'd never seen a playground in his life.

"You okay, kid?" I asked him, as I considered my options. I could leave him here to fend for himself and his likelihood of survival would be slim to none or I could take him with me and my likelihood of survival would drop exponentially. The kid shrugged, seeming not to know what I expected him to say.

"Are you hurt?" I asked, after which, the chubby kid shook his head, wide eyed.

"Where are your parents?" I asked him a third question that seemed important at the time. The kid's face became red and he began to look as if he wanted to cry, pointing a thick finger toward the way I had come. If they'd been out in that mess, they likely hadn't survived. A split decision was made and I motioned for the kid to get up. I gave him the bag to carry, hoping a task would take his mind off of what had become of the store and the way his life now seemed to be.

"Come on then, let's get what we need and go." It wasn't the time for pleasantries, we needed to get out of here in case the monsters tried to come back for another round.

The internal storage area had barely been touched, at this time. Boxes and boxes of unmarked, untouched packages that hadn't had time to be stocked on the shelves. These would be gone eventually, but for now they remained in tact. Having stocked the shelves of the store at one point in time, I knew what to look for and found things fairly easily, packing the bag with items of use. Knives, a set of pots that fit within each other, things that, though they might not be of much use to anyone who would catch us on the street, were of great importance to our survival at the moment. By the time I had filled it to the point that I was satisfied, it was much too heavy for the boy to carry.

"Let's go." I glanced toward the front of the store, with which the boy glanced with me, we both frowned and I shook my head.

"This way." Making my way even further toward the back, I tried my key card to open the door. No power, the generators had run out or broken down and there was nothing left to get the door open. Glancing around I weighed my options again. In the end, it was easy to figure out what I needed to do.

"Stay with the bag." I spoke to Geary without looking back toward him, focusing on my new mission.

Throughout a person's life one imagines what they might need in an emergency situation; food, water, weapons. These things are essentials for survival. It wasn't until this point that I even realized how much I took for granted. From the electronic doors that were blocking my way to the outside, right down to the thought that once I was outside and in the world, I'd realized during the walk back to hardware, I had no way to even start a fire were I in need of one. Which, we all learn, as quickly as first grade, is also a basic, caveman-esque need. As six year olds, we know how a caveman cooked his food, that six year old will tell you that he cooked it on a fire. I had no idea what rested beyond the walls of this store, but had seen the kind of carnage that had become of the isles here. A carnage that had no resolution after three days. My adult mind could only imagine what had become of everywhere else. A package of lighters was easy enough to pocket on my way to grabbing a small tool kit.

I ripped it open haphazardly as I made my way back toward where I'd left the kid, though of course, he wasn't to be found when I got there.

'Damn kids.' I remember thinking to myself, glancing around the area, having hoped that he had simply waddled off nearby. Of course not. To be completely honest with myself now that I'm writing it down, I might not have went looking for him, if he hadn't dragged the bag of supplies that I had gathered together moments ago with him. Though, it also made the kid easier to find, as the bag had left a track behind him in the rubble of the store.

I'm not sure why I hadn't noticed it before, maybe it had been the initial shock that was now being won over by annoyance and a sense of determination, but it was at this time that I noticed a particular smell that lofted its way toward me. Though I had only smelled something similar a few times in my life, I knew instantly what it was. The smell of death, of decay, the rotting not only of the food still remaining on the shelves, days after the generators had killed the refrigerators, but of those poor souls that had been caught in the tomb that was now the grocery section of the store. Yet, even after this smell began to assault my nostrils, the path of the sports bag led further. It led past the glass coolers, doors wide open, curdled milk spilled over the floor, now dry and cracked with a few days time. Its odor beginning to fade, especially with more overpowering smells lingering in the air. The trail led past shelves of dry rice and beans, of which, it was obvious were left for more easily cooked and flavorful foods. Though I made a mental note of what remained on the shelves as I moved along, in case I had the need to eventually return. For now, my sense of heroism had been peeked and my main goal was focused on getting the kid to safety.

Once again, to be completely honest, I don't know that getting the kid to safety was as much for his sake as it was for my own. However, only while writing the words out on paper now, do I realize it hadn't truly been the goal from the very first time that I had met Geary. Now, I can look back and realize that if I had truly had Geary in mind all along, I should have probably just clubbed him over the back of the head right there and then and let that be the end of it. Hindsight though, as they say, is twenty-twenty. At that very moment, I had convinced myself that getting him to safety was for him, when in truth, it gave me a goal. It took my mind off of the situation at hand and instead provided me with a mission and a feeling of purpose. It provided a way to keep my thoughts from drifting to my family, friends, the state of the world as a whole, the future, all number of things that had coursed through my brain before I had happened upon my young ward.

It wasn't long before I had found the kid once more, enough time that the damage had already been done. There he stood, at the edge of the sea of bodies, that puddle of violence so grotesque that even I, as an adult, had a hard time glancing at for more than a moment. There he was, staring forward, seeming unable to tear his wide eyes from it. Considering the state of video games and movies before the collapse, one would think that the youth of that day might have been immune to such sights, but then I suppose it is completely different to get the full effect in reality. The smell was worse than the sight, it held thick in the air, like a putrid syrup that one could taste and its flavor was just as terrible as the smell. Again, I could feel the bile rising in my throat, as quickly as I could I grabbed the bag from the boy, and ushered him away.

I'm not really sure just how long he was in shock, he stared forward blankly, as if when his eyes had fallen over the casualties a piece of his soul had seeped out. It seemed like it took forever for me to pull the door off of the hinges, without electricity the locks couldn't be opened, and being unsure what the outside world might hold, going out the back door was probably our safest plan of action. I tried to make the least amount of noise possible, not concerned for the moment about the kid that hadn't moved from where I'd left him. He'd barely even blinked. I knew he was in a non-responsive state of shock, but maybe it had been better that way, I had hoped at the time that he'd be able to block out these moments and when society got a handle on things once again, he'd be able to forget. I wouldn't forget. I wouldn't be that lucky. Especially as a writer, to this day, I can remember and describe every moment in great detail and as much as I am trying to provide a detailed account of these days, there are some things that are better left unsaid. The bloody isles of the grocery section is one of them. I society wouldn't come back as easily as it had fallen. If the last seven years is any indication, the human race might not ever truly recover. That year might have been the beginning of the extinction of our species. Unfortunately, for Geary, blocking out the memories of these events would not be an option.

Part 2 - The Outside World and What Happens When a Nation Falls

The Sun was bright when I finally pulled the door away from the frame, squinting as if it might help me see better with the light beaming on my face. I hadn't even realized that it was daytime, as without the lights, the store had been a dark and shadowed dungeon of many horrors. The back lot was empty, save for a few vehicles, likely of employees who hadn't been nearly as lucky as I had been. I hadn't even been to the very front of the store, I could only imagine what I would have found there, likely it would have been much worse than even the isles of gore we'd already seen. Likely what we saw was only those whom had made it through the first round or two. Even then, it was obvious to me the state of things. I kept alert, telling myself that I wasn't going to let anything bother me, no matter what I might see outside. The kid followed me blindly, without any sort of emotional reaction, it was as if his body moved out of instinct rather than choice. I could tell that at the very moment, no one was home inside of his head, the scared kid had left him for the time being and he followed me moreso because he had no other choice. It was follow me or be left behind and for now, we didn't have the luxury of fear.

Strange enough, when I opened that back door, I almost

expected to find littered corpses polka dotting the landscape, but instead there was nothing. For as far as my eyes could see, everything looked the same as it had been three days ago. Three days ago, when I had come outside to smoke a cigarette, bored with life and unsure where exactly I wanted to go from here. Looking back on those days before, everything that I had considered seems so trivial, all my concerns meaningless and shallow. My senses still perked so as to notice any sign of movement or life, I carried the bag toward one of the vehicles, motioning for the boy to follow me. I wasn't exactly sure what I intended to do once I got there, I'd never hot-wired a car, I didn't know how to start it without a key and so my eyes moved over them searching for something, anything that might put me behind the wheel of a working vehicle.

It's moments like these that seem to put your life and how you've lived into perspective. If I hadn't have gotten that second DWI a month before, I might have drove my own car to work, but as it stood, my vehicle sat in my parent's driveway and I had caught a ride with a friend. I cursed myself for being an idiot, though obviously I couldn't have known at the time that I would be in dire need of transportation, that I could end up in a life or death situation without the aid of a vehicle. The subdivision was too far to go on foot, especially for the kid, who looked as if he was beginning to get sun-burnt just from waiting on me to make a decision. I took a deep breath. I shielded my eyes from the sun, looking in the direction of the front parking lot. So far, we'd not seen an actual threat. We'd seen the aftermath of a disaster, the remains of a battle for survival, left so haphazardly that one wondered if there were even anyone left to clean up the mess. Or maybe they just didn't care. I tried to keep my mind from wandering away from my goal, instructing the kid to hide under the box trailer of a semi truck while I went around the front to try to find us a car. Everything was quiet, too quiet. What normally might have been a midday rush at the store, was soundless and void. The sound that was missing from the scene almost deafening and it caused my ears to begin ringing from lack of stimulation.

This was now the third time I had considered walking away from the boy, but still my morals stood firm. As far as I knew, he had no one left in the world. Likely his parents were somewhere in that mess of bodies, a fact that I was sure he knew. Had he been an adult, I probably would have left him and not thought twice about it, but for some reason seeing that kid alone and scared hit a soft spot.

The front parking lot told a story, from beginning to end, a timeline of events that, being a writer, played out like a tiny movie inside my head. I was glad I had left the kid behind. It was also at this time that I knew the world had changed and not just with the lack of technology, but that civilization was gone. With the layers of the timeline, the stages of the dead that I could see, each act became more ferocious, more animalistic and primal. The desperation close to the end of the struggle was apparent and, as it seemed, not that long had passed. My eyes scanned the parking lot. I saw no movement, but that only offered a small amount of consolation, because as I quietly made my way through the vehicles I wasn't finding any that were of use. Doors had been left open after their owners had been slaughtered beside their vehicles, the batteries long since dead after days of sitting open. My imagination considered what that first night might have looked like, the car lights dimly lit like fireflies in the parking lot, the backup generators of the store still keeping everything going. Rivers of fresh blood from that initial struggle, the panic that had ensued just before I had ducked out of sight. I couldn't have imagined then just how bad it had gotten, in fact, even as I made my way through the rows of unusable transportation, I still hadn't a clue just what the world had become. Even at that point, it was merely a hint of the atrocities that I would face in the years that followed.

It took me a while, but eventually I found a car. It wasn't the optimal situation, as it's previous owner hadn't made it to even opening the door, having been hit by what looked like a stray bullet. I was thankful that the old man had died with the windows cracked, because a hotbox of death would not have been as easy to tolerate. I reached inside the window and pulled open the manual lock, opened the door and allowed the lifeless body of the old man to stiffly pour out. I tried not to think about the emotional implications of the situation, kept myself from thinking of the man as a person and instead I thought of him as merely a necessary obstacle. There wasn't anything I could do for him now. There wasn't anything I could do for any of these poor saps. Not now anyway and if I had tried before, I would likely be rotting along with them as would the boy. I pulled the body of the man out of the way, so as to not run over it when I pulled the vehicle out of its parking spot. As I sat in the driver's seat of the station wagon, it reminded me of my grandfather, the white station wagon that took him and my grandmother everywhere and the way he always smelled like Rolaids. I had never understood the obsession that the elderly had with Rolaids. Minty antacids. Who really cared what it tasted like, as long as it did the job. To me they always tasted like minty chalk, but in my youth anything that had a sweet flavor and I could get away with was fine by me. It hadn't mattered that it was medicine, it hadn't mattered that it tasted like chalk, what mattered was that it gave me that sense of satisfaction, obliging my sweet tooth and, in my own mind, I felt like the adults were none the wiser.

It felt so strange to sit there soundlessly thinking about my grandparents, having lost them years before. Yet, the natural death of two elderly people still affected me so much more than the masses of corpses around me. As I turned the key and the car roared through the silence, I wondered what that said about me and if I was the same as whomever had torn through all of those people. If their thoughts had started out just as mine had, with a numbness to the pain and suffering of others or if the numbness only came from the idea that the dead were beyond my help. After all, had anyone else helped the boy? In the beginning, there wasn't any way a single person or even a handful of people could have prevented the violence that ensued. But now? After the initial weeding out of those that were weak willed or weak minded, those that wouldn't have made it on their own anyway, were these the few that were worth saving or, for that matter, was anyone worth saving? If I left the kid behind, would he make it on his own? As I drove the car into the back parking lot, I somehow knew that I was his only hope of making it through, again picking up my mission of 'saving' the boy. I hadn't yet become the 'sheepdog' I am now. However, by that point, it was clear to me that it wasn't my choice who lived or died, what was my choice was who I became in this new world. Would I be just like those I had despised in those days before the lights went out and tear the world down with my own selfish desires, following the uncaring masses, thinking that I wouldn't make a difference? Or would I pave my own way, as I had always done, following my own heart, mind, and moral code of ethics? After all, in a lawless world, which was clearly what had befallen our nation, it isn't the man who speaks the loudest that survives, it's the man who decides that he isn't going to simply stand there and yell.

Chapter 3

Part 1 - Where We're Going, We Don't Need Roads

The sun was beginning to set by the time I pulled the station wagon around to the back where the boy was. Curled up in a ball, his arms holding onto the bag I had told him to watch for dear life, as if it were his savior. I couldn't imagine what was going through this kid's head before I came along and when I had left him to find transportation. He'd likely heard his whole life not to trust or go with strangers and now the only person he had to rely on was someone who he'd never met in his whole life, someone who barked orders, but rarely spoke otherwise. It hadn't been my intention, but it was something that I had realized as the boy crawled out from under the trailer, dragged the heavy bag to the car, and tried to lug it into the back.

"It doesn't have to be perfect." I said to him, trying to have patience with him and keep my tone as calm as possible. The boy simply nodded and shut the door as soon as he was sure the bag was clear of it. He hopped in the front seat, instinctively putting his seat belt on and staring straight forward.

As I put the car in drive, I wondered what I should say to him, or if there was even anything I could say to him that might ease his mind in the slightest. The likelihood that he was alone in the world was fairly high, considering the state and place I had found him, unless he had extended family somewhere, but in that case it would mean getting him there and, for tonight, he needed somewhere to lay low, rest, and recover from what he'd been through. Hell, even I needed that, at this point.

It was within these moments, just the two of us, alone in the car, that I realized that the boy hadn't said a single word since I had met him. I felt slightly responsible for the non-congenial way that things had went and I tried to soften my expression, it wasn't easy considering everything that was going through my mind at the moment, but I convinced myself that I had to for the sake of my traveling companion and my own sanity.

"Do you have a name, kid?" The question was straightforward and simple, I expected to get an easy answer from him. However, for the time being, I was only met with silence, as the kid kept staring forward at the passing landscape.

"You can call me Luc." I told him, hoping that if I was friendly with him he might open up a bit, but he seemed unresponsive still. I frowned. I wasn't sure how to handle the situation. I didn't have any kids of my own and hadn't really spent much time around them, other than the random children that came and went from the store.

It wasn't long though before we were met by our next obstacle. I could see it well before we truly reached the massive congestion of empty vehicles, left behind for one reason or another, but this scene, much like the parking lot, had its share of horrors. It certainly wasn't something a twelve year old should have seen, but then for the time being, this was the world we lived in. I contemplated my options, as I slowly inched forward on the highway. In truth, there was only one decision I could make.

"Hold on, kid." I told him, before whipping the wheel to the right and taking the station wagon off-road. The kid's eyes got wide and he grabbed onto the door, as the car bottomed out and jumped along through the grass. We were lucky that most of this was flat lands and as the crow flies, we weren't that far from our intended destination. It was my first instinct to go home. I wasn't sure what I would find there, but I had to go. Hopefully my family had been intelligent enough to protect themselves and hold down the fort during the three days I'd been gone, but as I kept pushing forward in the direction of the suburb where my parents house lie, nestled right in the center of upper-middle class society.

I could tell that the kid was not used to off-road driving and while in a straight away, I tossed him a half smile, forced as it was, I hoped it would calm him a bit. I was sure he probably thought I was insane by now, but what other option did he have at this point? It was either me or he was on his own. He was old enough to realize he wouldn't last long by himself, especially with those out there that committed such terrible acts as we saw at the store and in the traffic jam. However, both scenes made me wonder just how much of the world was like this. What percentage of the world had fallen and what still remained? At this point, I was sure that not everything had fallen, there had to have been parts that were guarded by military or that police control had held strong. All along I had wondered what exactly had happened to take down the entire grid, what kind of threat can bring down a nation in one swift blow. Of course, it wasn't truly the person who took down technology that had committed those heinous acts that I had seen. It had been normal people, the same people that I had seen come into the store day after day, desperate to survive in a world that they didn't know how to live in. They hadn't been taught beyond what they could buy at the store or the bill companies they paid every month. That desperation had turned into the violence we saw, the fear that they would not survive this black out, in the end it was that fear that destroyed them.

Part 2 - Plausible Deniability and the Development of Wolves

After a few minutes, we pulled into the driveway of my parents' house. I glanced toward Geary, whom was still staring blankly out the window. I then looked toward my childhood home. It seemed untouched and, for that moment in time, gazing at it almost made me feel as if everything was still the way it had been.

"This is it." I once more turned my attention to the boy, however for some reason my eyes remained fixed on the house in front of me. Maybe it was because I wasn't sure what we would find inside. Were my parents still there? My brother? Had what happened reached this far out? I thought about it for a bit, then directed my next statement once again toward Geary.

"Stay in the car for a few minutes." Without moving his head from watching out the window, he nodded. I was beginning to wonder whether or not this kid could speak at all, considering he hadn't said a single word since I'd found him. I sincerely hoped that he could, considering I had no understanding of sign language whatsoever.

"Alright then, lock the doors behind me. I'll come back and get you if it's safe." Once again the boy nodded. I promptly slid out of the vehicle, reluctantly dragging my feet toward the door, my mind a flutter with thoughts of my family and of the kid that I had left in the car.

I didn't knock on the door or announce my arrival in any way when I walked inside. I wasn't sure if I was walking into a field of daisies or a hornet's nest. Little did I know, I probably should have compared the experience to falling down Alice's rabbit hole.

"Luc!" My mother happily greeted me from the kitchen. I could smell the most amazing fragrance coming from where she was, as she began to walk toward me, wiping her hands on a towel. She didn't seem shaken at all. As if, as far as she was concerned, beyond these walls everything existed as normal.

"Where have you been, honey? I've been worried sick." She paused for a moment, before giving me her assessment of the situation, which held no comparison to reality.

"I was afraid you'd went on another bender or shacked up with some woman for the last couple of days." She rolled her eyes and shook her head, as if she were disappointed with me because of some normal reasoning for my absence from the house.

"I can't imagine that you were with a girl, considering..." She made a face at me and my physical appearance. There I stood, wearing the same clothes I'd had on three days ago. I was sweaty and likely smelled. My brown hair greasy and separating itself into unwanted clumps of chin-length masses. I was dirty and exhausted, but determined. Though, the expression on my face had slowly become confused as I realized just how oblivious she was to the world outside of this house. At this point, I wasn't sure whether she truly didn't know what was going on or if she was merely choosing to block out what was happening and go on with her normal routines, as if nothing were the matter.

I watched her in silence for a few moments, as always, buzzing around the living areas of the house like a hummingbird flitting in a field of hibiscus.

"Go get washed up for dinner, honey." She paused for a minute and stared blankly out in front of her for a moment, before pulling herself from her own thoughts. "Your brother is out with friends and..." She stopped again, seeming to shuffle through her mind, before looking toward me. Her expression had a twitch to it that I had never seen before. "Jacob won't be joining us either...he's been spending a lot of time in the garage lately."

Something was wrong with what she was saying. Nothing about this situation seemed rational, as if she expected to wake up from this life into the life that she was accustomed to.

"Mom, where's Chad?" I couldn't have cared less about where the hell my step-father was. He could have fell off of the face of the Earth and it wouldn't have made one bit of difference in my life. However, my younger brother was a different story. Even though, at times, we didn't get along, he was still my brother and I was concerned for him.

"Oh, he went with friends." My mother once again stared into the air, as if something that I wasn't privy to were playing out in her mind. She leaned against the arm of the couch she was near, as if she might fall if she didn't. My eyes scanned her appearance, making note of differences and the blank expression that kept forming on her face. It was in that moment that, with her hands clasped in front of her, I noticed the red marks on her wrists. It was obvious that she had tried hard to hide it. I knew, even at this very moment, she was trying to convince herself that it was all just a nightmare.

"Mom, where's Chad?" I repeated myself, grabbing a hold of her out of instinct, against my better judgement. I didn't accept her answer, as she was very obviously in shock and not thinking clearly.

"Mom." I raised my voice a bit and gave her a small shake as I tried to bring her mind back to reality for a third time. Her eyes were empty as they stared into mine. This close to her I could see the effects of the last couple of days written all over her face. Eyes puffy and bloodshot, the effects of continuous crying and lack of sleep.

I let her go slowly, still staring at her. She slumped backward into the couch, her whole body seeming to give up, as her mind fell silent. I watched her. She wasn't my mother anymore, she was the shell of my mother, left over from an experience unknown to me at this time. I moved away from her, keeping her in my peripheral vision, as I made my way to the garage. She'd said that Jacob was spending a lot of time in there and Chad had went with friends. A part of me knew that it was probably a version of the truth, I was sure that my mother had decidedly blocked what had actually happened from her conscious mind.

The Testament of Lucifer

(NOVEL START [UNFINISHED - POSSIBLE FUTURE] - 2018)

Disclaimer From the Author: This novel is purely a work of fiction and not intended for any purpose other than to entertain. It is not divine inspired and, while some parts of it may be based on theology, was not meant to portray any historical accuracy whatsoever. I did grow up within the church. This is not intended to be blasphemous, prophetic, or even taken seriously. This novel simply attempts to ponder what might be a different perspective and/or angle on theology. Please don't burn or protest my book. If you don't like the idea of it, don't read it. I am not a supporter of evil, nor am I a worshiper of Satan.

I am an artist, my words are my paintbrush, I would like to color your mind.
For those that are still with me, thank you and enjoy.

"Thou [wast] perfect in thy ways from the day that thou wast created, till iniquity was found in thee." - Ezekiel 28:15

"And the devil that deceived them was cast into the lake of fire and brimstone, where the beast and the false prophet [are], and shall be tormented day and night for ever and ever." - Revelation 20:10

Preface

"Since the very beginning of recorded human history, I have been deemed the beast, the betrayer, evil personified, the devil. While these accounts were mostly fabricated and untrue, those worthy of the truth would have never listened and those whom might have listened were unworthy. What about the Satanists, you ask? With incorrect information as their guide, they worship the idea of Satan that humans created, an imaginary entity built over time to be the greatest evil there ever was. Although, in a way, it is somewhat flattering, the written word of the church couldn't be further from the truth, as I have seen it." Lucifer paused the digital recorder he held in his left hand, after which he dropped his hand to his side, looking beyond the cliff on which he stood, toward the horizon. After a few moments, he closed his eyes, remembering the land in front of him the way it had once been and not the way it was now. The beauty that once was his father's greatest creation, now drowning in metal and plastic.Without turning his head or continuing his recording, he once again spoke out loud, as a figure walked up behind him, breaking his solitude. "Where should I begin, brother?" He paused, once again beginning to stare into the distance. "Should we go all the way back to Genesis? Maybe even further? Or simply skip ahead to save time?"

"You don't have to do this. You know as well as I that humans do not actually want the truth. They want the fantastical. Everlasting life, stories of miracles, someone to blame for their wrongdoings, the promise of salvation." The figure stepped up beside Lucifer, matching his gaze out over the land in front of them. "Those of the faith will deny any authenticity in what you tell them, the atheists won't even pick it up to read, and the Satanists would end up reexamining their beliefs." His voice almost held a melodic tone, but just beneath the surface of that voice was tremendous strength. His appearance was very young, seeming as if he couldn't be older than his mid-teens, however his eyes exposed him. Golden curls framed his face, somewhat resembling the halos that had depicted them as holy throughout time. His clothing was fairly contemporary, considering the boy was older than time itself. He slid his hands in his pockets, holding them there as he once again continued. "We know the truth. So what if some of the details are askew? The survival of the written word all this time is a miracle in and of itself. Besides, you've never approved of our Earthly brothers and sisters since the dawn of creation. What's made you change your mind enough to care about what they think of you?" The boy turned to his brother, watching with slight curiosity.

Lucifer still watched the blinking lights of the city in the distance, answered the boy without yet looking toward him. "I haven't...and I don't." He stopped only for a moment, seeming distracted, however trying to participate in the conversation as much as possible. "It's coming, Michael. The end. Revelation. It's already begun." Finally he turned to his brother. "The horsemen are at the ready, waiting for His command. Rumors of the return of Emanuel circulate within the Abyss faster than I am able to keep up with them." He turned his eyes back to the world in front of him. "As far as I am aware, there is no truth in these rumors, especially considering I have not fulfilled the prophecy to father a child of my own." Though, even as he said this, he knew that action on his own part wasn't truly needed, if the Father wanted the holy wars to begin they would. "Humans are parasites on this world, but they should know the truth before they are forced to pick a side."

Michael nodded lightly, before patting his brother on the back. "There is no harm in trying, I suppose." The young man took a deep breath. "Though, their salvation or damnation is ultimately up to them. Their fate does not affect yours, you have served your penance, when the war begins, your punishment ends." He shrugged. "You're under no obligation to save them. He will take the chosen, the rest must survive judgement." Michael turned, walking back toward the way he'd come. "If you insist on going through with 'The Gospel of Lucifer', start at the beginning. Our beginning." With that, the boy threw his shoulders back hard, forcing his wings to spring out like an umbrella behind him. "Oh..." He glanced back toward his brother for a moment. "...and make me look good." He gave his brother a smirk, then bent his knees, before shooting to Heaven like a speeding bullet.

Lucifer watched Michael leave, before turning his gaze back to the scenery, once again speaking to himself, however he didn't turn the recorder on just yet. "The beginning. That in and of itself is a long story, let alone basically rewriting the Father's biography." He lifted the recorder in his left hand up, staring blankly at it for bit. "Michael's right. I have to start at the beginning." After all, without the beginning there would be no end, or anything in between, for that matter. He pushed the record button and once again continued to record his account of history as he knew it. "In the beginning, Father created the Heavens and the Earth..."

1

In the beginning, Father created the Heavens and the Earth. Thus begins the book of Genesis. On that first day, when the Earth was created, the Father looked down on his creation and there was only darkness, emptiness, and so, out of that nothingness he bore to the Earth its first gift of life. However, within that first attempt he saw imperfection. When He created these first creatures, he watched them and within these creatures he saw far too much power, far too close to his own existence; and so, it was in an attempt to break down this power that He split these creatures. These first creatures were broken into two separate entities, one of darkness and one of light. The division of these creatures that was dark and evil of nature he named Demon and gave them dominion over the night. The creatures of light and goodness, allowing them dominion over the day, he called this division Angel. He looked upon what he'd created within that first day and was pleased. However He'd come to the realization that His world needed something more. With this knowledge in mind, He rested, leaving His first creations to attend to His world while He slept.

In the book of Genesis, all of this takes place within a day's time; however, one day for the Father is far more than the human mind is capable of understanding. At that time, for us, His immortal creations, it was one day because the Father called it one day. Looking back, in comparison to a day within the life of a human, it was actually a time span of many years. Within these years our Father was resting, the angels and our demon counterparts cared for His world, as we had originally been created to do. The days that followed, the angels praised the Father for his creations, admiring Him more with every blessing He had given to this world. Though, with each new life form we discovered, both Angel and Demon kind were given more and more responsibility. The more obligations that sprang forth on the Earth, the further Demon kind strayed from the wishes of our Father. Angels remained faithful, still praising our Father for the gifts he bestowed upon the world. However, it was not to last. For it only took a single entity, the last of which He gave, to begin the rebellion.

Up until the birth of mankind, the Father had favored me, His most cherished son, Lucifer. I had never before questioned His creations and had always remained in awe of Him. I had went above and beyond the tasks given to me and earned my place within the hierarchy of my kind. Even then the ranks of angels and demons existed, performing tasks in direct correlation with each position. Whereas I stood in a position of great esteem, I became the messenger between the Earth and its Creator. That also did not last long.

It was the sixth day that some of us, the Father's first children, began to question His plan for the Earth. That day, He created animals on the land that, though they were alive and shared some of the same traits with Angels and Demons, they were very clearly different in almost every way. Once again we stood in revelry at these new life forms. These, second only to the two divisions of the original creatures, were by far his greatest creation yet. We immediately began caring for them, as we had always done. Little did we know, while we were distracted by our duties, the Father created one more race of being. He exalted these beings as perfection and held them in even higher regard than His immortal children. Demons were the first to react to this new life form, abandoning all responsibility they had been given. They felt betrayed and angry at Him for crafting a creature almost identical to his first born. They cursed the Father and rebelled against Him. Though, this was only the first battle, it was far from the end of the war. Angels, while we also felt hurt by this creation, respected the Father and were charged with driving the Demons away from His paradise and into an abysmal void, created to imprison them for all time as punishment for their traitorous acts. It was during this time, while once again we were distracted, that our dominion over the Earth was taken from us and given to man.

When the Angels returned triumphantly, the Demons successfully imprisoned in the void, we beheld a sight that shocked and confused us. The world that had been ours, long before man was created, we were expected to leave and happily hand over complete control. Some Angels did as they were told, obediently joining the Father in the heavens. Others, like myself, could not understand the reasoning behind His actions. We began questioning our Father's judgement, trying to understand why He would give so great a gift to such inferior creatures. The gift I speak of here, was not the land nor the creatures of it, the gift was that of himself. Our

Father gave of himself to these creatures, something given to none of his other creations. Even further still, it was not given to the entire species of man, merely these two.

As I had been His favorite, it was I that spoke to Him directly, the voice of all those among my brothers and sisters that also needed clarity.

I believe, if I had been any other Angel, the outcome might have gone a bit differently. However, the Father and I spoke casually about the situation. I voiced our concerns of man's ability to properly care for the world and the fear that the rest of His creation might be destroyed by these simple minded creatures. He assured me that these humans were innocent and could not be corrupted. In addition, even though our kind had done well while charged with this task, we would always be one half of a whole. I didn't believe Him. It was true that Angels and Demons had been split from one original form, but I was convinced beneath the exterior perfection, something about these humans did not sit well. Sensing my apprehension, even though I dared not voice it, He offered to test them, not only to prove to me but also any others that may have had their doubts. With this, I was grateful and satisfied. If these creatures passed the test, they truly were all the Father had said they were, if not, it would show Him that He should return the Earth to Angel control.

As promised, Father devised a test for man. He touched the Earth and from His touch a tree began to grow. He spoke to the male and female He'd given the world to, telling them that all was theirs, except for a single tree. This tree and the fruit it produced were forbidden, not only were they warned against eating this fruit, but they were not to even go near this tree. He then returned to the Heavens to await the conclusion of the test He'd given them. I, however, wanted a closer view of what transpired, so I disguised myself as a creature of the garden. I had always thought the serpent powerful and cunning, also small enough to hide among the branches of the forbidden tree. I watched them closely, knowing that they would not be able to resist temptation. I wanted to prove to Him that these creatures were not His chosen, I wanted to show Him that we, His elder children, were much more fit to reign over this world. I was not surprised with how quickly the two to approached the forbidden tree. I watched them as they inspected this new tree with curiosity. I saw the craving in their eyes as they looked upon the beautiful fruit that grew from it. With a burning jealousy consuming me, against my better judgement, I whispered to them, still hidden within the tree. I planted ideas in their head of how delicious the fruit looked. I told them that the Father would never find out and that a single bite wouldn't hurt.

Exactly as I had predicted, the female reached into the tree, pulling a single piece of fruit from it. She inspected it for a moment, admiring its beauty, then brought it to her lips. She took a large bite from it, the juice within the fruit escaping and dripping down her chin, savoring the flavor of the fruit that was unlike any other within the garden. Though slightly more resistant, the male took the fruit when it was offered to him by his mate. He too took a large bite from the fruit, his expression changing from suspicious to one of gratification and enjoyment. Before either could take another bite, the all powerful voice of the Father spoke to them chastising them for their disobedience. I felt vindicated and righteous, silently congratulating myself, thinking I had proven my kind to be the better caregivers of this world. However, what the Father did next had not been a part of my plan. He did not remove man from control, instead He cast them from the garden and punished them with mortality.

Shocked and dismayed, I returned to my brethren, informing the Angels of what had happened. We became a race divided. While some trusted in the Father's plan, others were just as outraged as I. These creatures had proven themselves unworthy and yet were still the favored of all of His children. Over a short time, this divide deepened, until both sides were so angry we could no longer live at peace with each other. It was this divide that caused the revolt, which in turn gave birth to a civil war within the Heavens. It had not been my intention to cause a war, brother against brother and sister against sister, but whether I'd wanted it or not, it had begun. The shame I felt had been immediate, but I kept it hidden, putting on an air of strength for those who had chosen me as leader of the rebellion. After all, of every Angel in the Heavens, I had been the closest to our Father. I had seen the humans betray Him and I had watched as He forgave them. It was an injustice, but we should have known better than to challenge the Creator and those who remained loyal to Him. Our war was over before it even began and all those who had opposed Him shared in the same damnation.

The Legend of House Draco

(SHORT STORY – SHOCK FICTION - 2019)

Fog as thick as molasses rose over the horizon of Welhallow's Gate. The crimson banners of House Draco flying high over the barriers of the city, a warning of the blood ram to all who dare question the authority of its Lord. The city carried an eerie calmness, seeming lifeless through tyrannic enforcement of curfew, its Lord master holding fearful his people. The city wasn't always the savage prison it was now, holding captive its residents with a bloody, iron grip. However, for the last hundred and fifty years the Draco family had held its position, fear spread far and wide, so much so that none dared attack the city or the castle.

Auric Draco poured over his newest conquest pacing through the doldrums of the night at its peak. Blade in hand he sliced through flesh, searing through with a sizzling hiss. The muffled screams of his victim, hung from steel hooks descending from the ceiling within the belly of the castle, echoed on the stone walls. A monstrous grin fell over the face of the young man, adding a piece of tissue to the collection he'd already placed over the fire pit near him. He didn't speak to his captive. Chattel weren't worth his words and they were all worthless in his eyes. His flaying knife pierced one of the grilled slices, bringing it toward his lips, and blowing the heat from it, before he took a bite. The young man savored the flavor of his work, closing his eyes as he enjoyed his meal. He'd perfected the art of keeping his food fresh and to his liking. He'd learned the exact age in which harvest should be done and which methods left the meat tasting its best. Terror basted the flesh with the spice of adrenaline that filled it with flavor and a moistness that enhanced the savory disposition. Over the few years of his rule he'd produced the lottery that kept his palate to his specific liking, but it was the mandatory renewal of those resources that had maintained his household's customs over the generations. His was not the first of the Draco line to be cannibalistic in nature, in fact House Draco was known for its brutal lineage and rule. However, each new Lord had his or her own specific tastes when it came to their prey.

Auric's happened to be young adult in nature, as he hadn't the stomach to flay a child and past a certain age meat tended to be rather tough. Though he also had a reputation for even more brutish practices than that of most previous rulers, all known well, but mostly unspoken for fear of retribution. By the time he was finished with each food source they begged for death with mumbled words that could no longer be understood through tongueless mouths and sewn lips. Their eyes seeping tears from stitched eyelids. Tender bits were among the first to be taken, delectable in either gender of humanoid swine. As it stood, this was the second night of harvesting from this particular body and so it wasn't his favorite meal of this week, but it would certainly do, especially considering the other resources within his dungeons were slightly tapped out for the moment. The lottery was due soon anyway, a new unfortunate chosen once per week. This particular month three had perished before their time, causing him to be short a few meals and having to make do with what few morsels he had. He'd been impatient and had caused the creatures to go into a shock state that had ultimately lead to death, a rather amateur move on his part.

Auric could afford to be a murderous, cannibalistic monster. His rule was absolute, feeling no necessity to wed nor produce an heir at the time, he cared little for having another person to answer to. Not that there were a string of volunteers with his reputation, however that suited the young man just fine, considering. Another stifled shriek reverberated through the room once more as he stripped off another piece of the hanging creature's hide. Creature as it now was, considering the gender could no longer be told, scarring covering any pertinent attributes that might have constituted a human being. The outcries were like music to Auric's ears, enjoying every bit of the process of excoriation of the body. He knew he would have to cease his actions soon or he would cause the heart of the being to falter and ultimately fail. He needed this individual to last at least another round or two of cultivation, as after the selective draft he'd need at least a couple of days to a week to exhaust the physical worth of the chosen, a process in which he thoroughly enjoyed.

Auric picked up a clean rag off of a spotless counter near him, wiping the flaying knife of any substance that might have been left behind from his dinner. He then sat it down and wiped his hands with the same towel. Picking up a silver plate and fork from that same table, he pulled the remaining slivers of flesh from the small grill, and covered it with a lid that would stifle the fire within. Fare in hand, he walked away from the gruesome sight of the hanging monstrosity, his footfalls moving away, the being seemed to relax, shaking from the wounds it had suffered, however thankful that the slicing away of its flesh had finally ceased. Auric left the grisly scene for a servant to clean up, having tired of the avocation and making sure to perpetuate the possibility of future meals gained from the livestock. He consumed the meat as he walked, setting down the dish and utensil on a random table, uncaring as to where he laid it, making his way toward his quarters. Though he would soon retire, last week's draft recipient awaited his arrival.

Closing the door behind him, his eyes fixed on his prize. He'd been working on this one for days now and the girl's assets for the purpose of his own gratification were almost exhausted. They were of course his favorite, though young boys were not beyond his spectrum of satisfaction, it was all the same to him. The female's head hung, arms tied at the wrists above her, her form exposed so the young Lord could make use of her as he saw fit. Small cuts and bruises lined her body, as Auric was not exactly a tender partner in any way and the young woman knew what horrors awaited her when he'd tired of this particular use of her. Auric placed his hand on the warm skin at the girl's hip, allowing it to slide up her bare frame, lingering only momentarily on elements of her that he deemed arousing. Moving behind her, his grip ultimately winded the entirety of her hair within it, jerking her head backward, causing her back to arch, and the girl to cry out in pain. He held the girl's hair tight as he pulled her close to him. This week she was a girl and a plaything, next week she'd be just another food source. Regardless of how he utilized her, they all served a purpose, they all served their Lord and fed his needs. Auric liked to think them fortunate. After all, what could be better than to give of themselves for their sovereign leader?

The Ballad of Willie Shade

(SHORT STORY - SHOCK FICTION - 2019)

The rugged Jeep sputtered to a halt in the most inconvenient of places, in the middle of Bum the Fuck Egypt, New York. Rich had been driving, Jay asleep in the front passenger side, while Willie had been in the back seat, feet up and reclined, on the bench, sucking the life out of the vehicle's battery beating the same level in Angry Birds he had beaten a million times before in the last three years. Obviously the phone hadn't any service any longer, no one called, no one texted, but the playlist and games on the frequently dead cell phone were invaluable to him.

"Will..." Rich spoke, staring ahead toward the dimming headlights in the darkness. Willie didn't answer, still focused on the game. "WILL." Rich spoke a bit louder, still no answer. "WILL!!" This time Rich didn't take anything to chance and a hand reached back and smacked the man-child in the back seat.

"What, man? What?" Willie seemed annoyed to be disturbed from his game, however catching the lack of brightness of the lights ahead of them. He slid his feet around, placing them on the floorboards, standing up, and staring ahead of them. "Well son of a bitch..." Willie kicked the back of the seat, waking Jay up with a startle. "Hey shithead, did you remember to put gas in this beast before we left Ohio?" Jay blinked a couple of times, seeming to try to get a bead on what the hell was going on.

"Fuuuuuck..." The voice from the passenger seat groaned. "Man, I knew I forgot some shit like that. We lit the fuck out of there so fast though, man..." It was true, Willie tended to either piss people or the Wasted off wherever he went, it was a wonder the other two hadn't left him behind yet, however as many times as the young man tended to get the three of them into trouble, somehow he had also gotten them out of it.

"Well, that settles it then..." Willie started, sliding the phone into his back pocket, letting his eyes adjust to the dim light of the dying headlights. "...piss break, then we're hoofing it, boys." Willie jumped out of the Jeep, the modified guitar strapped to his torso, as it always was. The other two men also deciding to jump out of the Jeep, however staying much closer to the vehicle than Willie seemed to care to.

Willie had always been the one going off on his own, the loner, the brave one, the leader, the creative mind, the man with a plan...to be honest, it was just that Willie hadn't given a shit less before the outbreak hit nor after. Of course he cared about his brothers in their little band of misfits, but the rest of the world could burn in hell for all he cared. The apocalypse suited him just fine so far, he never had cared about the fans and without the need for money in this new world, he had no use for adoration or an audience any longer either.

The moon was enough light for Willie to make his way quite a distance from where he'd been, listening around him for any sounds of footfalls or rustling in the grass, before unzipping to relieve himself of the half a gallon of water he'd consumed during the long ride.

After he'd finished his business, Willie turned and began

the walk back toward where the lights of the Jeep still barely shined in the darkness, beginning to zip and button the worn and faded denim jeans as he walked. However, his attention was caught after a short moment, by the crunch of foliage, and the too familiar quiet growl of the undead. A wide and almost insidious grin grew over Willie's face, as he slowly turned toward the sound. He could tell the difference between them now, having studied the sounds of the vocal cords as their growling reverberated in their decaying throats. He mind combed through the sound profiles that he'd filed away in his head. The mere sound of the growl told him several things about the creature, the way it moved toward him told him others. He could tell it was mostly in one piece, by the way it barely made a sound as it moved over the grass. It was alone, as far as he could tell. Feminine voice pattern, not long undead by the sound of mere faint elasticity of the lifeless resonance that it's throat uttered in it's grotesque call. It was a the sort of call that Willie listened for frequently, but rarely was able to find in such a world as they lived in these days. These days, one had to make do with what one could get.

"Come here, doll..." Willie whispered, one hand sliding the Frankenstein of a guitar that he carried around his body, to where it sat in a more normal positioning for such an instrument. Willie poised himself as if he were hunting the creature and not the other way around and it didn't take them long to find each other. The female Wasted was smaller than he was, but seemed fairly similar in age, if not possibly slightly older, it was often hard to tell because of the expression of death shadowing their features. Willie was careful with his attack on the being in front of him, having done the same act quite a few times before, knowing exactly how to make the most of such an occasion. With one swift thrust of the base of the guitar, he hit the soulless woman hard enough in the side of her head to knock her spinal column lose, but not to kill her. "This is going to hurt me a lot more than it is you, Liz." He called them all Liz, after his most recent ex, before the world fell to shit. Reaching forward, Willie grabbed the thing's hair, thankful it didn't fall out as he did so, as it would have been a bit more difficult if it had. He'd certainly been there before, almost bitten by a damn Liz. He used quite a bit of strength, to force the dead girl's head around, without severing the delicate nerves that connected the brain to the rest of the female's body, before nudging the creature to the ground. "Oh yeah, not a bad catch, Willie boy." Willie knelt to the ground, pushing the creature's biting face into the dirt with one hand, and tugging on his still partially undone jeans with the other hand, letting them fall around his knees. "Don't worry, babe. Being dead is excellent birth control."

After quite a bit, Willie came walking back to the Jeep, making sure he was zipped and buttoned, his guitar once more slung around behind him. Rich was back in the driver's seat waiting semi-impatiently, Jay was leaning against the side, arms crossed over his chest, a cigarette hanging from his lips.

"That was quite the piss." Jay spoke through holding tight to the cigarette. The two were quite aware of Willie's 'quirks' and though it wasn't often spoken between the three, the thought of doing what they knew their leader had just done, creeped the two other young men right the fuck out. Jay shifted forward, grabbing his own monstrosity of a modified bass guitar and his thickly stocked backpack from the seat behind him.

"It's been quite the drive." Willie retorted, knowing exactly what his band-mate meant by that. Rich just grumbled a few inaudible things, grabbing his own bag, and beginning to slowly walk forward on the road, Jay following close behind, while Willie quickly took his own bag from the back seat and caught up with them, walking a few steps behind. He lit a cigarette of his own, seeming to have a complete lack of remorse for his previous actions, if not having almost completely forgotten about it already. However his brothers knew and kept their eyes on the road ahead, having seen the remains of Willie's extracurricular activities on previous occasions and had no want or need to relive viewing such atrocities.

"So where did they say this place was at back in Ohio?" Willie spoke up, breathing out a breath of smoke. It wasn't long before they passed the motionless mound of a corpse that Willie had left behind, the man himself not even glancing toward it, the other two averting their eyes intentionally. The body had been left behind, put out of its misery by a single stab wound to the back of the skull, now in the front of its body, however, seeming out of mere routine Willie always ripped their heart from their body. Whether it was out of pure rage or pain or simply a complete numbness in his soul, Willie left his grotesque and undeniable calling card. "Well guys..." Willie spoke almost with a playfulness to his tone, throwing his arms around his long time best friends, now on either side of him. "...where's our next stop?"

MEANINGFUL QUOTES

(Random Thoughts Throughout the Years)

The Quotes

Advice from the broken: Fall swiftly and silently, hit every branch on the way down, and when you look up...regret where you are, but never regret the fall. (2008)

Ysmim - The ability to stay joyful when you're screaming inside. (2008)

Mopping - The process in which one smears wet dirt evenly across one's floor. (2009)

I flip a coin to make up my mind...but every time it lands on it's side...waiting on the wind to blow it over... (2009)

Shine down into the shadows of my mind so that I might see a brighter day... (2009)

When it doubt, keep a look out, the answer will shine through the darkness of confusion... (2009)

Tension floats in the air, cut it with a knife, see how it slices, everywhere you go, the cruel mist surrounds you even when you're alone. (2009)

Tick tock, the sands of time fall grain by grain, I'm buried in the drifts, unable to escape the waves that blow against me...somehow I need to break the cycle. (2009)

It's not my job as a parent to judge their blood, but to guide them as they are given an opportunity to judge for themselves. It's not my job to pass judgement on other people, but to keep my distance from those who have shown me that I should be skeptical. It -is- my job to survive and to help bring peace to, not only my life, but the lives of others. I just hope I have the strength. (2009)

I don't need happily ever after to fall for my Prince Charming...my life isn't a fairy tale, by any means, but all I ask is someone to treat me like a princess. (2009)

Life is a paradox, every part of you wants to follow your instincts, except your brain which feeds you that bit of doubt that overpowers everything else. Why is everything so complicated? I'm ready for simple pleasures in my life, I'm tired of the complicated messes I seem to always be in. (2009)

Premonition, precognition, chills run down my spine... the cold outside feels as if it's seeping in, as I calm my worrying mind. Convincing myself that the moon will return again... Be safe dark knight, keep your light bright, while you're out my sight tonight. (2009)

Grey skies turn to black, luminating with countless sparkles littering the darkness...this is home, a feeling that I am never alone. Forever would I fall into that clear ocean of sky, held by the gentle embrace of my Moon. (2009)

When day breaks into the wee morning hours, the suns rays bringing light to the world, will I wake to that familiar insecurity...or will I begin anew like those rays that pierce my darkness? Sing sweet dear morning birds for it could always be your last. (2009)

Because the temptation of the moonlight lingers in my mind like a warm and familiar flame...but the temptation of the sun blinds me into icy cold submission. (2009)

We all sound the same You don't know my name Rearrange and things don't change Things remain, feel the strain Stress, catch my breath (There'll be a new tale of) Get some rest (He and I) From the mess (In fact any time) I couldn't care less (Every day) These are the words of Tricky...in my own words, I'm tired of some of this crap that I am so addicted to. Why can't I get away? Tomorrow is another day, but it doesn't matter when I think it will probably just go the exact same way. I need to disconnect, this connection that has rose color pulled before my eyes. My best friend, my internal conflict, reasons why my mind tells lies. (2009)

Sometimes it hard to define, whether the truth is really in my mind and the reality I see with my eyes tells me lies...or if I'm crazy and my brains all hazy seeing things that must be make believe...these things that are so unclear to me... (2009)

Life's simple perfections are yet to be a part of me, somehow these pleasures have drifted too far to see, troubled waters wash away and won't let be, these simple things I try so hard to see inside of me... (2009)

If you could bend the reality in your world, what would you do? If you could make your dreams come true, would it become your nightmare? *As an artist, I bend my own reality and most of what I see are nightmares...does that say something about my own world or does it say something about everyone else's?* (2009)

You are my temporary high, when I'm with you I can touch the sky, my addiction, my affliction...my curse is that I can't figure out why, when I'm not by your side I feel so cold and dry, seeing you always brings me back again, waiting for a fix that never ends, this one is for you my drug, my friend.. (2009)

"I love you," is the most complex, sacred thing that a person could ever say, because love is more than an emotion, more than a feeling...it's a pull from one person to another, a knowing that this person is a part of your future, for however long, the knowledge that...if it came down to it, you would step in front of a bullet. (2009)

Because the walls that you didn't know were broken, need to be recemented. Because the wounds you mended are bleeding, torn again unintentionally. I hid some things from you, because I was scared to lose everything. I will remain in the shadows, because that's where I'm comfortable. You scare me because you make me feel happy, when nothing else does. (2009)

Some of the best artwork is done in secret, with the intention of showing no one. The best inspiration is the soul's truth that forces itself out, because you can't contain it any longer. I know my weaknesses and I'm working on them, someday I will let that sketchbook be seen...until then, my artwork collects. (2009)

The King of Swords has spoken...his advice heard but hesitant on my part. Not because it isn't what I want to hear, but because my mind is so chaotic and my heart is so guarded... I am the Ice Queen. Portraying a warm facade, until it's time to let someone close...maybe Spring should come again in my life. Hopefully that ice isn't too thick to melt...and if it is able, it won't melt into complete vulnerability. (2009)

The moon shines around my shoulders, even after I have left for the day. The thought of that illumination makes me smile as I make my way. My lunar love, I wish I could have you for my own. I reach out often to grasp your light, but in the morning, still wonder if next time I might hold you. My comfort remains, but also my hope...another night you might see what things could be if you were next to me. (2010)

The moon shines around my shoulders, even after I have left for the day. The thought of that illumination makes me smile as I make my way. My lunar love, I wish I could have you for my own. I reach out often to grasp your light, but in the morning, still wonder if next time I might hold you. My comfort remains, but also my hope...another night you might see what things could be if you were next to me. (2010)

Sometimes even ice has to melt into tears, even though it seems as if the world was just as cold today as it was yesterday...the frozen eventually melts into a puddle of what once was. It was just time for the rain. (2010)

When the Ice Queen stares into the mirror she sees sadness and beauty, strength and solitude. She rejects those who try to warm her temporarily, but finds solace in understanding. Do not mistake her silence for emotion unspoken, consider it contemplation, a warmth rarely shown. She wouldn't waste her time on the unknown, her motives her own. Assumption the greatest path to destruction, misunderstanding to corruption. (2010)

...because the world should hate me for being who they want me to be and love me for who I am underneath...tired of wearing a mask for those who don't understand and would rather I just be 'normal'...don't you see? Normal is killing me... (2010)

I'm lost, don't try to save me, there is no map to where I have come and back to good. This jungle I wander tears at me with vines of thorns, I can't escape their grasp. So dark, the treetops cloud the future and the past, making me so unsure of where I'm going, knowing...I can't go back, but looking forward to more pain. (2010)

I am starting to think that those with a -true- artist's soul are not meant for a 'happy' life...it has come to my attention that my inner turmoil breeds my best work. In other words, I may always prefer to be alone, but in my world, I create my own happiness...it's not mandatory that anyone else understands. (2010)

In my mind's eye, I soar on high, in bright blue skies, with a sigh, I fly...until the ground beneath me begins to dry, it cracks with heat it fries. As much as I try, I can't help but wonder why...amidst such a beautiful day, in the end, on the scorched earth I lie... (2010)

Never judge life by what you do for others or what they do for you...life lies...judge it by looking beneath the surface to inner core of everything around you...only when you see what is hidden will you truly find peace with yourself and others. Also, make sure to pay attention to the present and consider what you have, before looking onto the future and what dreams may come eventually...if you ignore the present for hopes of the future you may miss something that you don't realize you already have...because realizing it in the future may be to late... (2010)

When one road ends, another begins. The smooth roads you look back on with a smile, remembering the nice drive...the bumpy roads you tend to be glad you moved past them. While you would drive the smooth roads again, if it were the direction you were going...you figure out ways to go around the rough ones. Here's to my pavement and rocks. (2011)

In very few situations things are as they seem...there is always something more to be told, something more to say, something that you might not have known if you didn't ask questions. Live with suspicion, for knowledge is power. Question your world. (2011)

I am crazy. I am a mess. I am my own thoughts. I will confess. But I am my music and I am my art...I dance in my own world with all of my heart. To some it means nothing, to me everything...waiting for someone to hear the song that I sing... (2011)

I don't believe... Mindless mockery... Unfortunate when the dreamer falls out of love with the dream, but when what was wasn't.... Isn't anymore, never again... Standards high, expectations low, follow the dreamer into the darkness... Dream no more. (2011)

Love is -not- about who you can tolerate to be with...it's about who you can't tolerate to be without... (2012)

Humanity needs to be taught to be human again...we are now the closest thing to biological robots as we can be. We rely on electricity and man-made energy so completely that most would be lost without it. We conform to orders so quickly with no question as to right and wrong. We are the zombie nation...a nation of flesh coated, hive minded robots... (2014)

The basis for humanity starts at home. You can not expect to change the world if you do not first change yourself... (2014)

"We hold these truths to be self-evident, that all men are created equal, that they are endowed by their Creator with certain unalienable Rights, that among these are Life, Liberty and the pursuit of Happiness."

Remember this quote as you go through the day...too many people feel as if the world -owes- them something or they -deserve- more. No one is entitled to anything. You are entitled to your life, your freedom to live that life, and you are able to pursue happiness...pursue. That means that you are entitled to the ability to -work- for your happiness, that does not mean the world needs to give it to you...

Pursue your happiness today. (2014)

It is my opinion that, in life, there is a designation of three separate, but equally important stations of people. These stations are Warriors, Muses, and Expendables.

Now, the Warriors in life are the doers. These are the people that get things done. They are not always particularly bright and are often times stubborn in their views on it. They work day to day for the days to come, with little thought or worry of the distant future. They are those that make things happen in life, much of the world as we know it can be attributed to the Warriors, they wage war against life and most of the time win their battles, because it is their whole purpose to do so. These people are very likely to try very hard their first time and if they fail they are done, like the great Yoda said, "Either do or do not, there is no try."

Then there are the Muses, these are the dreamers, the

philosophers, the inventors. They are not necessarily very active or physical, they sit around thinking what could be and worry about what might be some day, figuring out how to solve problems and usually inspiring a Warrior to take action. Their sole purpose in life is to create ideas, sometimes they might put them into action, but usually they fall right back to their station after. They might try and fail over and over, but they keep going forward, pushing for a new day, one where their ideas might be put into fruition.

Then there are the Expendables. These people, though they seem as if they are useless, are actually a very important part of the world. They are your extra bodies. Though this station is not particularly good for the Expendable themselves, they are very important for the Warriors and Muses. They are also there for service, while the Warriors and Muses are busy doing what they do, the menial tasks of the world still have to be done, they are those that hold these positions.

For Example, that hot blond in a horror movie, someone has to die...this is what she is good for, she is always the first, because the doer is the hero or the heroine- they are the survivor...the Muse, although they are full of ideas on who the killer might be and how they might survive, is not always so good at accomplishing these things, it is always the lone Warrior that survives. In an example outside of the movies, that hot blond uses her services in other ways...possibly to inspire the Muse or in 'service' of the Warrior.

I consider myself a Muse in life, though sometimes you may not know exactly what station you are truly in and at times I may have a Warrior's spirit, I always generally fall back into my station...today's thought to think about, what station are you and what is your purpose? This is one thing that makes life worth living...to have a purpose. Find yours. (2015)

Machines do not account for human free will...

Never fully rely on a machine, its functions are definite and we as human beings are undefined... (2015)

How you handle life's struggles defines who you are...are you a lion or a mouse? A deer or a tiger? Will you go quietly into the darkness or will you kick and scream until you bring yourself to the light? (2015)

Miracles happen every day, sometimes we're just too clouded by judgement to see them... (2015)

I do not believe in hocus pocus magic. I believe that the souls of some are just more evolved than others. I believe 'true magic' comes from within...the older and more experienced that soul is, the more powerful it is as well. However there gets to be a point in time when the spirit of an 'old soul' wears out, begins to deplete energy faster than it can receive it... Let your soul shine bright every day and push yourself just a little bit further, let the magic within your mind, body, and soul fill those of others with that 'magic'... Every day of my life, I have let that magic flow like a river into every thing I do and it is my heart that leads the way. Blessed are those who bless others and expect nothing in return. Blessed are those who sparkle and shine with that magic...the reward for this never comes in any way that you would expect, but it's there, if your eyes are open. Watch for your signs every day. May Fate bring you all nothing but wonder and magic in return. (2015)

About the Author

My name is Charity Gaff and I am an American author residing in Northeastern Missouri. I grew up on a farm 19 miles away from Kahoka, Missouri. I am married with two biological children and two bonus children. I enjoy being at home with my family and learning/practicing traditional life skills, such as: cooking from scratch, gardening, canning, sewing, crocheting.

Much of my young adult life was spent merely surviving. For most of it, I was a single mother working one or two jobs and trying to go to college while doing so. In 2012, I purchased my tattooing license and began doing tattoos. I quickly realized, however, that it wasn't an art that one could self-teach well, so I acquired an apprenticeship from a local shop. I apprenticed and worked as a shop manager within this shop for a couple years.

In 2015, I was diagnosed with Multiple Sclerosis. It was a

very rough year, before I finally went into remission in 2016. Due to this diagnosis, I spent much of that year in a deep depression. However, after several months of feeling sorry for myself, I decided that I was not going to let my disease define me. I picked myself back up, not only from the blow of finding out about the MS, but from a six-year relationship that did not work anymore and the tattooing career that I had been working so hard toward. With muscle spasms and the having had two seizures while my disease was active, I decided that I did not trust myself to put out quality tattoos. I resigned from my position at the shop and cancelled my tattooing license.

In 2017, when I had almost lost hope of happiness, I reconnected with someone that I had worked with in the past, Jeremey Gaff. We began dating and within a very short time, we moved in together. In 2018, we bought the house that we currently reside in and in 2019 we got married, officially bringing their family together.

I put out my first novel in the Spring of 2021. The Archives of Metaphysical Warfare was born. This first book had been a three year labor of love and I intend to create a long standing series with it. The second book of the series is planned to be published within the first part of 2023.

I received my Associate of Arts degree, graduating with honors, in May of 2022. My emphasis of study was creative arts and history. I am still undecided as to whether I intend on going any further with my education. I currently substitute teach in the town I reside.

My life has been littered with many struggles, some that I am not ready to put into words. Some that still haunt me to this day. Eventually I may put out an autobiography, however it is not currently in the works (though I have had many requests). This compilation of many different types of writing is the evolution of pain, despair, joy, and revelation that I have went through in the process of becoming a published author. Some may not understand, some may not see the value in these pieces, but they are parts of me, pieces of my life. I wanted to share them with the world, instead of letting them sit and collect dust in a file. I hope they are a benefit to those who read them. Thank you.

ALSO BY C. GAFF, THE ARCHIVES OF METAPHYSICAL WARFARE: VOLUME 1: THE END IS THE BEGINNING IS THE END IS AVAILABLE MOST PLACES PRINT AND EBOOKS ARE SOLD.

Published April 2021.

www.ingramcontent.com/pod-product-compliance
Lightning Source LLC
Chambersburg PA
CBHW061205210726
48294CB00006B/1761

* 9 7 8 1 7 3 6 4 7 8 9 5 0 *